Date Due

DE 1-9-83			

SELECTED POEMS

Louis Simpson

SELECTED POEMS

Harcourt, Brace & World, Inc.

New York

To Dorothy

Contents

NEW POEMS

THE ARRIVISTES

1949

Carentan O Carentan

Trees in the old days used to stand
And shape a shady lane
Where lovers wandered hand in hand
Who came from Carentan.

This was the shining green canal
Where we came two by two
Walking at combat-interval.
Such trees we never knew.

The day was early June, the ground
Was soft and bright with dew.
Far away the guns did sound,
But here the sky was blue.

Th[e sky] was blue, but there a smoke
[Hung still ab]ove the sea
Where the ships together spoke
To towns we could not see.

Could you have seen us through a glass
You would have said a walk
Of farmers out to turn the grass,
Each with his own hay-fork.

The watchers in their leopard suits
Waited till it was time
And aimed between the belt and boot
And let the barrel climb.

I must lie down at once, there is
A hammer at my knee.
And call it death or cowardice,
Don't count again on me.

Everything's all right, Mother,
Everyone gets the same
At one time or another.
It's all in the game.

I never strolled, nor ever shall,
Down such a leafy lane.
I never drank in a canal,
Nor ever shall again.

There is a whistling in the leaves
And it is not the wind,
The twigs are falling from the knives
That cut men to the ground.

Tell me, Master-Sergeant,
The way to turn and shoot.
But the Sergeant's silent
That taught me how to do it.

O Captain, show us quickly
Our place upon the map.
But the Captain's sickly
And taking a long nap.

Lieutenant, what's my duty,
My place in the platoon?
He too's a sleeping beauty,
Charmed by that strange tune.

Carentan O Carentan
Before we met with you
We never yet had lost a man
Or known what death could do.

Summer Storm

In that so sudden summer storm they tried
Each bed, couch, closet, carpet, car-seat, table,
Both river banks, five fields, a mountain side,
Covering as much ground as they were able.

A lady, coming on them in the dark
In a white fixture, wrote to the newspapers
Complaining of the statues in the park.
By Cupid, but they cut some pretty capers!

The envious oxen in still rings would stand
Ruminating. Their sweet incessant plows
I think had changed the contours of the land
And made two modest conies move their house.

God rest them well, and firmly shut the door.
Now they are married Nature breathes once more.

Song: "Rough Winds Do Shake the Darling Buds of May"

Rough winds do shake
　　　　　　do shake
　　　　　　　　　the darling buds of May
The darling buds
　　　　　rose-buds
　　　　　　　the winds do shake
That are her breasts.
Those darling buds, dew-tipped, her sighing moods do shake.

She is sixteen
　　　　　sixteen
　　　　　　and her young lust
Is like a thorn
　　　　hard thorn
　　　　　　among the pink
Of her soft nest.
Upon this thorn she turns, for love's incessant sake.

Her heart will break
　　　　　will break
　　　　　　　unless she may
Let flow her blood
　　　　　red blood
　　　　　　　to ease the ache
Where she is pressed.
Then she'll lie still, asleep, who now lies ill, awake.

Well, I have seen
                have seen
                                one come to joust
Who has a horn
              sweet horn,
                          and spear to sink
Before he rests.
When such young buds are torn, the best true loves they make.

GOOD NEWS OF DEATH

1955

The True Weather for Women

Young women in their April moodiness
Complain of showers, for they cannot go
Swimming, or to the courts to play tennis.
But if they suffer from a gentle blow,
What will the storm, the terror of saints, do?
If April presses their green tenderness
How will they stand the full weight of the snow?

Now they are killing time, with darts and chess,
And others dancing to the radio,
And some for kisses take a turn to guess
At names, and laugh at tales of love also.
Jenny, in her hot tub, repaints a toe,
Admiring her perfect nakedness
While thunders crack and summer lightnings glow.

There is one date that they will keep, although
They have been often late to come to men,
For death hits all such deer with his long bow
And drags them by the neck into his den,
And there eternally they may complain
And tap and gesture in a frantic show
And look at summer through a window-pane.

Wind up the pulse with poppy, sleep them so!
Their selfishness will always entertain,
And even death will seem small weather woe
When love is all their sun and all their rain.
The clock will never strike, adjusted then
To their sweet drowsings, and they will not know
How punctual death is, or else how slow.

As Birds Are Fitted to the Boughs

As birds are fitted to the boughs
That blossom on the tree
And whisper when the south wind blows—
So was my love to me.

And still she blossoms in my mind
And whispers softly, though
The clouds are fitted to the wind,
The wind is to the snow.

A Woman Too Well Remembered

Having put on new fashions, she demands
New friends. She trades her beauty and her humor
In anybody's eyes. If diamonds
Were dark, they'd sparkle so. Her aura is
The glance of scandal and the speed of rumor.

One day, as I recall, when we conversed
In kisses, it amused her to transmit
"What hath God wrought!"—the message that was first
Sent under the Atlantic. Nonsense, yet
It pleases me sometimes to think of it.

Noli me tangere was not her sign.
Her pilgrim trembled with the softest awe.
She was the only daughter of a line
That sleeps in poetry and silences.
She might have sat upon the Sphinx's paw.

Then is she simply false, and falsely fair?
(The promise she would break she never made)
I cannot say, but truly can compare,
For when the stars move like a steady fire
I think of her, and other faces fade.

The Man Who Married Magdalene

The man who married Magdalene
Had not forgiven her.
God might pardon every sin . . .
Love is no pardoner.

Her hands were hollow, pale and blue,
Her mouth like watered wine.
He watched to see if she were true
And waited for a sign.

It was old harlotry, he guessed,
That drained her strength away,
So gladly for the dark she dressed,
So sadly for the day.

Their quarrels made her dull and weak
And soon a man might fit
A penny in the hollow cheek
And never notice it.

At last, as they exhausted slept,
Death granted the divorce,
And nakedly the woman leapt
Upon that narrow horse.

But when he woke and woke alone
He wept and would deny
The loose behavior of the bone
And the immodest thigh.

John the Baptist

The Prophet, scourged by his own hand, progressed
Through wilderness inhabited by brutes
Whose hollow voices would not let him rest,
Feeding on honey-combs and cactus roots.

The leopard frolicked in her leafy marking;
A multitude of undetermined shapes
Walked parallel. He fled the wild dog's barking,
The buzzard's black umbrella and collapse.

And as he fled from white Jerusalem
"Make straight the crooked way!" would loudly cry,
And fled from people and discovered them
As shadows at the corner of the eye.

Against the gaudy red edge of the world
There came a caravan. The camels kneeled
Under the drivers' blows; the fires curled
And to and fro the white-robed Arabs wheeled.

Their melody the rocks replied again.
In veils and silver serpents at the fire
The women sinuated; the tall men
Danced arm in arm, apart from their desire.

A Negro, shaking like an epilept,
Beat with his bleeding knuckles on a gourd,
Two naked dancers in the circle leapt
Swinging a supple child across a sword.

Then, at a long-drawn bray from throats of bronze
A Roman legion rapidly debouched.
The drums, the piercing flutes, were stopped at once,
The dancers in a sullen silence crouched.

They carried on the column of their necks
The stone dome of the sky, their naked knees
Rolled out an iron street. Triumphant specks!
Their echoes had increased the silences.

A fearful discipline of little swords
And buckled mouths . . . The shields had shifted place
With the quick ruffle of an angry bird,
A slant of lances like one man's grimace.

They ruled the living and revered the dead . . .
These were the last reflectors of the sun
And carried him in purple and in red,
Their braying shadows rampant at the throne.

The Prophet for his supper parched the locust
And of her little burden robbed the bee,
And laid his hairy cloak beneath a cactus
On the bright margin of eternity.

And all his dreams were of a marshy pool
Where the old Vices ran with backward glance:
Ingratitude, and Gluttony an owl
With human face, pot-bellied Ignorance.

An idiot with slack jaw and soiled rump
Was led upon a leash by sister crones—
Blind eye, flat dug, and amputated stump.
And there were mountain nymphs as smooth as stones

That kneel for centuries beside the waters
Under the leaves in the Italian wind,
Vases of clear song, the swan-necked daughters
Turned by divinity without a mind.

A centaur plashed in dappled dignity
Balancing a statue on his withers.
The forest flocked with gay stupidity,
The hoofs of goats and fluttering of feathers.

There, double-rooted, dark and ominous
The Tree of Knowledge screamed her triple text.
A pigmy, with a quiver of long arrows,
A monkey's head, both male and female sexed,

Fled from the shadow of pursuing Wisdom,
From the stained spear and the destroying shape,
And all the gods were guttural or dumb
To see Man separated from the Ape.

But was this Wisdom, with a woman's face?
She was not Wisdom, for she followed dancing.
Her mouth was smiling, an unholy grace
Flashed from her hands and from her eyes fell glancing.

And lightly lightly went the dancer's foot,
And as she danced she dazzled through a veil,
And softly softly played an Arab flute,
And on his throne a king sat stricken pale.

The Prophet woke. The stars were large with rain,
The moon upon a cloud lay soft and bright,
The pagan fires smouldered on the plain,
The tiger swung his lantern through the night.

And to the valley's winding ways he ran
Crying "Prepare the straight path for the Lord!"
And came to shallow Jordan, where began
The matter of the platter and the sword.

Memories of a Lost War

The guns know what is what, but underneath
In fearful file
We go around burst boots and packs and teeth
That seem to smile.

The scene jags like a strip of celluloid,
A mortar fires,
Cinzano falls, Michelin is destroyed,
The man of tires.

As darkness drifts like fog in from the sea
Somebody says
"We're digging in." Look well, for this may be
The last of days.

Hot lightnings stitch the blind eye of the moon,
The thunder's blunt.
We sleep. Our dreams pass in a faint platoon
Toward the front.

Sleep well, for you are young. Each tree and bush
Drips with sweet dew,
And earlier than morning June's cool hush
Will waken you.

The riflemen will wake and hold their breath.
Though they may bleed
They will be proud a while of something death
Still seems to need.

The Battle

Helmet and rifle, pack and overcoat
Marched through a forest. Somewhere up ahead
Guns thudded. Like the circle of a throat
The night on every side was turning red.

They halted and they dug. They sank like moles
Into the clammy earth between the trees.
And soon the sentries, standing in their holes,
Felt the first snow. Their feet began to freeze.

At dawn the first shell landed with a crack.
Then shells and bullets swept the icy woods.
This lasted many days. The snow was black.
The corpses stiffened in their scarlet hoods.

Most clearly of that battle I remember
The tiredness in eyes, how hands looked thin
Around a cigarette, and the bright ember
Would pulse with all the life there was within.

The Heroes

I dreamed of war-heroes, of wounded war-heroes
With just enough of their charms shot away
To make them more handsome. The women moved nearer
To touch their brave wounds and their hair streaked with gray.

I saw them in long ranks ascending the gang-planks;
The girls with the doughnuts were cheerful and gay.
They minded their manners and muttered their thanks;
The Chaplain advised them to watch and to pray.

They shipped these rapscallions, these sea-sick battalions
To a patriotic and picturesque spot;
They gave them new bibles and marksmen's medallions,
Compasses, maps, and committed the lot.

A fine dust has settled on all that scrap metal.
The heroes were packaged and sent home in parts
To pluck at a poppy and sew on a petal
And count the long night by the stroke of their hearts.

The Ash and the Oak

When men discovered freedom first
The fighting was on foot,
They were encouraged by their thirst
And promises of loot,
And when it feathered and bows boomed
Their virtue was a root.

O the ash and the oak and the willow tree
And green grows the grass on the infantry!

At Malplaquet and Waterloo
They were polite and proud,
They primed their guns with billets-doux
And, as they fired, bowed.
At Appomattox too, it seems
Some things were understood.

O the ash and the oak and the willow tree
And green grows the grass on the infantry!

But at Verdun and at Bastogne
There was a great recoil,
The blood was bitter to the bone
The trigger to the soul,
And death was nothing if not dull,
A hero was a fool.

O the ash and the oak and the willow tree
And that's an end of the infantry!

American Preludes

This isle hath many goodly woods and deer,
Conies and fowl in incredible abundance;
The woods, not such as you find in Bohemia,
Barren and fruitless, but the highest cedars,
Better than those of Libanus, and pines,
Cypress and sassafras and lentisk:
To them the sea winds owe their wafting spice.

Discharging our muskets
A flock of cranes, most white, arose by us
With such a cry as if an army of men
Had shouted together.

We saw not any of the people
Until, the third day,
In a little boat
Three of them appeared, and one of them
Went on shore, to whom we rowed.
He attended
Without any sign of fear.

When he had spoken,
Though we understood not a word,
Of his own accord he came boldly aboard us.
We gave him a shirt,
A hat, wine and meat, which he liked well.

The next day
Came divers boats, and in one of them
The King's brother.
His name was Granganameo,
The King is called Wingina,
The country, Wingandacao.

The women wear their hair long on both sides,
The men on one; they are of color yellow;
Their hair is black, yet we saw children
That had very fair chestnut colored hair.

For an armor he would have engaged us
A bag of pearl, but we refused,
As not regarding it, that we might the better
Learn where it grew.

This discovery was so welcome into England
That it pleased her Majesty
To call this country Virginia.

II

A flag-blue day with scarlets of furled cloud
A fowler's morning in the water reeds
Here on a white horse comes the General
Shaking the green tatters with his drums
And tanagers out of the cherry trees.

A farmer's view cut up in cherry pies
The fowler packs tobacco in his pipe
The branches are pricked out in violet
The farmer turns the plough and jackdaws hop
The General tugs at his wooden teeth.

The new farm will not bear too much Satan
A sudden child peers out from cherry trees
At rumps and trumpets and the General
Going with a tight rein and aching jaw
To carve the Lion, crack the Lobster's claw.

III

The white walls
Undulate with sea shadows. In the fields
The cypresses stand up like somber flames,
And yellow roses tangle from the walls.

Vaquero, I have seen your ending days,
Looped in a lariat, dragged at the heels
Of the black horses.

Under the eucalyptus tree
There is the girl who waits for me,
Her brown feet stretched to the salt tongues of sea.

Cathedral, vessel of God, wait for me,
Where potsherds and faded roses
Are cast beside the wall, and cypresses
Weep, sad sisters.

Cathedral, vessel of the dead,
O cast off these white anchors, Miserere,
And spread your spinnakers Magnificat
Laudemus to the horizon!

Blessings perch there like birds,
Saints gather like gulls
For pecks of bread.
The bow is booming in the blood of Christ.

But she does not weep, she does not chant Miserere,
Her eyes are green as the shallow sea,
The one who is waiting for me.

                    IV

Hudson, come down from your leaf-stroked cascades,
Angry so soon to be encased in ice,
Gone is the Sleeping Man and gone
The steamboat floating upstream like a swan,
But the calm sleep that raised these Palisades
To new, majestic augurs still persuades.

Green in summer; winter, white and cold;
The softest season neither young nor old,
Which two red Indians bring in,
Pocahontas in her painted skin.

The last Elizabethans reappear,
Court orange and fool's yellow. The bright air
Rasps the hunter's lungs; he walks peak-capped,
Flanneled, rubbered, wrapped,
His pockets bulging with fat shotgun shells.

Maple and berry dogwood, oak, are kings.
The axe is lively and your pale palm stings
While Echo claps her hands on the bare hill.
The scene is clear. The air is chill.

West

for J. R. S.

On US 101
I felt the traffic running like a beast,
Roaring in space.

                    Tamalpais
The red princess slopes
In honeyed burial from hair to feet;
The sharp lifting fog
Uncurtains Richmond and the ridge—
With two red rubies set upon the bridge—
And curtains them again.

Ranching in Bolinas, that's the life,
If you call cattle life.
To sit on a veranda with a glass
And see the sprinklers watering your land
And hear the peaches dropping from the trees
And hear the ocean in the redwood trees,

The whales of time,
Masts of the long voyages of earth,
In whose tall branches day
Hangs like a Christmas toy.

On their red columns drowse
The eagles battered at the Western gate;
These trees have held the eagles in their state
When Rome was still a rumor in the boughs.

Early in the Morning

Early in the morning
The dark Queen said,
"The trumpets are warning
There's trouble ahead."
Spent with carousing,
With wine-soaked wits,
Antony drowsing
Whispered, "It's
Too cold a morning
To get out of bed."

The army's retreating,
The fleet has fled,
Caesar is beating
His drums through the dead.
"Antony, horses!
We'll get away,
Gather our forces
For another day . . ."
"It's a cold morning,"
Antony said.

Caesar Augustus
Cleared his phlegm.
"Corpses disgust us.
Cover them."
Caesar Augustus
In his time lay
Dying, and just as
Cold as they,
On the cold morning
Of a cold day.

Ægean

Where only flowers fret
And some small passionate
Bird sings, the trumpets sounded yesterday.
The famous ships are gone,
Troy fades, and the face that shone—
Fair Helen, in her tower—could not stay.

Where are the temples set
Their gods would not forget,
The trophies, and the altars? Echo, say.
There's no one any more
But Echo on the shore,
And Echo only laughs and runs away.

Though still the olive glows
Like silver, and the rose
Is glittering and fresh, as in their day,
No witnesses remain
Of battles on the plain
And the bright oar and the oar spray.

Mississippi

When we went down the river on a raft
So smooth it was and easy it would seem
Land moved but never we. Clouds faded aft
In castles. Trees would hurry in the dream
Of water, where we gazed, with this log craft
America suspended on a gleam.

The days were mostly pipes and fishing lines,
Though for a turn or two we had a king,
A Nonesuch with his royal monkeyshines,
But treacherous, for all his capering.
The naked wickedness of his designs
Brought on Democracy, a steady thing.

Steady but alarming. Rip-tooth snags
Are wrapped in smoothness like the tiger's hide,
And when she blows, chickens and carpet bags
Go roiling seaward on the yellow tide.
And Brady photographs the men like flags
Still tilted in the charges where they died.

The river is too strong for bank or bar,
The landmarks change, and nothing would remain
But for the man who travels by a star,
Whose careful eye adjusts the course again . . .
Still shadow at the wheel, his rich cigar
Glowed like a point of rectitude—Mark Twain.

If ever there were Mississippi nights,
If ever there was Dixie, as they sing,
Cry, you may cry, for all your true delights
Lost with the banjo and the Chicken Wing
Where old St. Joe slid on the water lights
And on into the dark, diminishing.

Islanders

Poetry has no place, still you must choose
A starting point—say, with the displaced Jews
Who come to this small park from the ends of earth:
They weep with sorrow and expect a birth,
Their gutturals disrupt the summer nights
While darkness slowly laps the river lights.
Their skins are wrinkled like fine handkerchiefs
Of Brussels, intricately stitched with griefs.
The wind that stirs their soft curls makes you cold
Thinking of Belsen and of Buchenwald.
Their tears obscure your Christ like candlegrease—
A swinging acrobat, no Prince of Peace!
Cry thief! Someone has stolen the true Cross!
Go to these Jews, accuse them of your loss!

Poetry has no place, but life is kind.
Revenge yourself on a girl—she will not mind.
A glossy, sulky one comes strolling by;
The loiterers compete to catch her eye,
But, even as you stare, she's whisked away
By a sport jacket and a new coupé.
Tonight when he brings her home—"Oi, from his place!"
Her father cries, her mother slaps her face,
She packs her bag while the children wail and shout,
Her father asks her where she's going—"Out!"
And that means America. She may go far
And hang over California like a star,
Returning with affection fierce as spite
To lavish wealth and set the old rooms right.

This tapeworm, poetry, won't make you fat:
It's time for supper at the automat.
Those faces are reflections of your own,

30

Faces that cannot bear to be alone,
Faces at whose back scream nightingales,
Faces that cannot endure the sound of bells . . .
Could they exchange their hopes—no, they will stare
Into their own, out in the dark somewhere,
Gulping their beans. Each at some point preferred
To live like this rather than say a word . . .
Was it "I love you" or another "Yes"?
Each is fascinated with some strange success.
Their lips move silently; they are living again
Some secret hour of familiar pain.

II

In streets that darken, sinister for miles,
You think of Egypt and the crocodiles.
These massive blocks, from which the sun has fled,
Remind you of the labors of the dead—
Dull pyramids, too large to be destroyed,
That, even ruined, could not be enjoyed.
The slaves are not devoted to their toil—
They gather sullenly, at dark recoil
As though from gods of which they are ashamed,
Propitiated, served, but never named.

I see you suddenly transfixed and caught
In traffic—pale and spectral as a thought.
They drive on curves of steel and swoops of stone
So fast their similes will find them gone.
They will not wait for you—they are not flowers
Or statues, but the masks of worldly powers.
Like stars at speed they dream in a bright coil,
Their brains are glitterings, their blood is oil,
They have no past, they call their souls their own . . .
But time eludes them, time, and time alone.
They're in a tearing hurry, to enrich
The undertaker and to spoil a ditch.

III

I see you standing in the square called Times.
The lights spell out Adventure, Passion, Crimes,
Dances of Bali, Hitler's Loves, The Whip,
And sometimes Shakespeare for your scholarship—
Immediate seating, smoking in the rear . . .
The moon is blazing like a sign for beer.
To those who have been nourished on the swarm
This is a hayride, harvest on the farm.
Here come the handsome, and the rich, the smart
Arrive in Cadillacs that shake the heart—
The thief, the pimp, the actress and the whore—
Arabia, to the astonished poor.

The blind man counts the nickels in his cup,
But eyes go flying sideways, flying up
Like dazzled birds. Besides the daily wage
They're caught in their own lives, the inner cage,
And cry for exits, hoping to be shown
A way by others, who have lost their own.

And yet, seen from a distance and a height,
How haunting are the islands of the night,
The shores on which we dream, with the deep tide
Of darkness rushing in on every side . . .

IV

And you, an islander—listen! There it moves!
The sea reminds you of your early loves.
This is a liner of stone, with star-cleaving funnels,
These streets are the decks, we crowd to the blazing gunwales.
Look up at the men who paint a precarious mast—
The scaffolds are tossed by the wind, they hold carelessly fast,
They walk in the clouds, they gaze into blue gulfs of ether . . .

If you too stood in the storm, exposed to the weather,
In the pulse of sound and silence, wafting westward you might
    see

Another Aphrodite tiptoe on the white-curled sea.
If you could cast the moorings of the bridges and set sail,
Feel the waves of time go under, clinging to the sea-wet rail,
To meet her as she comes again, as once to Cyprus' bay,
A slender, golden figure riding on an edge of spray,
On the horses, the blue horses, that with curved necks come to
    meet
The horses, the white horses, that stand still on foaming feet—
And as she comes still closer you can feel the ocean swell,
And through the blue cathedral a percussion like a bell . . .
The city tilts and founders in a turbulence of gulls,
The waves regurgitate their fish, torn nets and splintered hulls,
And with one wind all will be drowned, to be God's bellyful,
Until with shining weeds enwound they rise more beautiful.

You find yourself at the Circle. This is no masted ship!
Those towers are the stalagmites of stars that slowly drip—
Flowers freaked with blue and white on stalks that seem to twist
To some great height where love is made and birds sing in a
    mist—
One rose, pistilla of light with red cloud petals,
Rose of the heart hammered thin, of the most precious metals—
A chisel driven aslant, a silicate wedge . . .

Enough of these images—they set the teeth on edge!
Life, if you like, is a metaphor of death—
The difference is you, a place for the passing of breath.
That is what man is. He is the time between,
The palpable glass through which all things are seen.
Nothing. Silence. A syllable. A word.
Everything.

        After your death this poem occurred.
You were the honored fragments from the Greek.
After your death these stones would move and speak.

A DREAM OF GOVERNORS

1959

The Green Shepherd

Here sit a shepherd and a shepherdess,
He playing on his melancholy flute;
The sea wind ruffles up her simple dress
And shows the delicacy of her foot.

And there you see Constantinople's wall
With arrows and Greek fire, molten lead;
Down from a turret seven virgins fall,
Hands folded, each one praying on her head.

The shepherd yawns and puts his flute away.
It's time, she murmurs, we were going back.
He offers certain reasons she should stay—
But neither sees the dragon on their track.

A dragon like a car in a garage
Is in the wood, his long tail sticking out.
Here rides St. George, swinging his sword and targe,
And sticks the grinning dragon in the snout.

Puffing a smoke ring, like the cigarette
Over Times Square, Sir Dragon snorts his last.
St. George takes off his armor in a sweat.
The Middle Ages have been safely passed.

What is the sail that crosses the still bay,
Unnoticed by the shepherds? It could be
A caravel that's sailing to Cathay,
Westward from Palos on the unknown sea.

But the green shepherd travels in her eye
And whispers nothings in his lady's ear,
And sings a little song, that roses die,
Carpe diem, which she seems pleased to hear.

The vessel they ignored still sails away
So bravely on the water, Westward Ho!
And murdering, in a religious way,
Brings Jesus to the Gulf of Mexico.

Now Portugal is fading, and the state
Of Castile rising purple on Peru;
Now England, now America grows great—
With which these lovers have nothing to do.

What do they care if time, uncompassed, drift
To China, and the crew is a baboon?
But let him whisper always, and her lift
The oceans in her eyelids to the moon.

The dragon rises crackling in the air,
And who is god but Dagon? Wings careen,
Rejoicing, on the Russian hemisphere.
Meanwhile, the shepherd dotes upon her skin.

Old Aristotle, having seen this pass,
From where he studied in the giant's cave,
Went in and shut his book and locked the brass
And lay down with a shudder in his grave.

The groaning pole had gone more than a mile;
These shepherds did not feel it where they loved,
For time was sympathetic all the while
And on the magic mountain nothing moved.

I Dreamed that in a City Dark as Paris

I dreamed that in a city dark as Paris
I stood alone in a deserted square.
The night was trembling with a violet
Expectancy. At the far edge it moved
And rumbled; on that flickering horizon
The guns were pumping color in the sky.

There was the Front. But I was lonely here,
Left behind, abandoned by the army.
The empty city and the empty square
Was my inhabitation, my unrest.
The helmet with its vestige of a crest,
The rifle in my hands, long out of date,
The belt I wore, the trailing overcoat
And hobnail boots, were those of a *poilu*.
I was the man, as awkward as a bear.

Over the rooftops where cathedrals loomed
In speaking majesty, two aeroplanes,
Forlorn as birds, appeared. Then growing large,
The German *Taube* and the *Nieuport Scout*,
They chased each other tumbling through the sky,
Till one streamed down on fire to the earth.

These wars have been so great, they are forgotten
Like the Egyptian dynasts. My confrere
In whose thick boots I stood, were you amazed
To wander through my brain four decades later
As I have wandered in a dream through yours?

The violence of waking life disrupts
The order of our death. Strange dreams occur,
For dreams are licensed as they never were.

A Dream of Governors

The deepest dream is of mad governors.
—MARK VAN DOREN

The Knight from the world's end
Cut off the dragon's head.
The monster's only friend,
The Witch, insulting, fled.
The Knight was crowned, and took
His Lady. Good and gay,
They lived in a picture-book
Forever and a day.

Or else: When he had sat
So long, the King was old
And ludicrous and fat.
At feasts when poets told
How he had shed the blood
Of dragons long ago
He thought, Have I done good
To hear that I did so?

The chorus in a play
Declaimed: "The soul does well
Keeping the middle way."
He thought, That city fell;
Man's life is founded on
Folly at the extreme;
When all is said and done
The City is a dream.

At night the King alone
Went to the dragon's cave.
In moonlight on a stone
The Witch sat by the grave.
He grasped her by the hand

And said, "Grant what I ask.
Bring evil on the land
That I may have a task!"

The Queen has heard his tread;
She shuts the picture-book.
The King stands by the bed.
In silence as they look
Into each other's eyes
They see a buried thing
That creeps, begins to rise,
And spreads the dragon's wing.

Orpheus in the Underworld

Night, dark night, night of my distress—
The moon is glittering with all the tears
Of the long silence and unhappiness
Of those who loved in vain for many years.

And so it glittered on the sleeping town
When Orpheus alone and sadly went
To death, to fetch Eurydice, and down
The fearful road pursued his dark descent.

Here were the walls, the gates where death had set
His warnings—in a city carved in stone
The citizens were busy; farmers whet
Their scythes in meadows never to be mown.

The kings and judges sat in their high places.
Then, at the sound of a loud trumpet blown,
They crowded, with pale terror on their faces,
From Death ascending to his dreadful throne.

Orpheus entered. As the eery light
Dwindled, he grasped his lute, and stumbling bent
His footsteps through the thick, enshrouding night.
Then suddenly, the lute by accident

Was struck—the sound exploded like a star
And shone and faded, and the Echoes woke
And danced, and ran before him. Down the far
Corridors it seemed the silence spoke.

He touched the strings again, began to play
In the same order. Fearfully he went
Toward the Echoes, and they still gave way.
And so he followed his own instrument.

At last to the deep hall of death he came.
And there the King sat, motionless and dread.
The night coiled from his nostrils like a flame;
The eyes lacked luster in the massive head.

And by his icy feet, pale in her shroud,
The beautiful Eurydice was laid.
Orpheus knelt beside her, and he bowed
His head, and touched the lute again, and played.

Night, dark night, night of my distress—
Once by the Mediterranean in May
I heard a nightingale, and the sadness of roses
In the murmuring wind, but this was sadder than they.

Night, dark night, night of my distress—
I too have waked her, seen the heavy shawl
Of night slip from her shoulders, and the darkness
Fly from her open eyes. And through the hall,

Through cities and the country of the dead
With the one I loved, hand in hand, have gone.
The dog of death was quiet as we fled,
And so we passed, as shadows over stone.

Under the hills in their enormous silence
And by the sea where it is always still,
I felt her hand in mine, the fearful sense
Of mortal love. And so we fled, until

I turned toward her. With a cry she vanished.
Goodbye, pale shadow of my happiness!
I to the light have been forever banished
That is the night, the night of my distress.

Then Orpheus pursued his lonely way
Upward into the world, and a strange glory
Shone from his face. The trees, when he would play,
Were moved, and roses wept to hear his story.

It's Orpheus in the wind. His music grieves
The moon. He tells the water of his loss.
And all the birds are silent, and the leaves
Of summer in that music sigh and toss.

The Flight to Cytherea

There are designs in curtains that can kill,
Insidious intentions in a chair;
In conversation, silence, sitting still,
The demon of decorum and despair.

Once, when I felt like that, I used to go
Abroad. I've made my marches drunk on night,
Hands in my pockets, pipe sparks flying so,
A liner to the tropics of the light.

Night is the people's theater, sad and droll.
There are the lovers, leaning on each other;
The businessmen, out for a little stroll
With their success; the bum who calls you brother.

And then, I've flown. I've risen like a sail,
A plane—the roads beneath shone bright and bare—
A black umbrella cracking in the gale
Over an ocean blank as a nightmare.

And came to Paris. I'm not talking of
Your chestnut blossoms, but the soldier's town,
The Butte, the calvados, odors of love,
Where for a little while I settled down.

In Africa I was. Beneath my wings
The lions roared. I floated on tobacco;
I made the eyeballs of the savage kings
Roll up. I spent a fortune at Monaco.

Then off again, to heights where the air fails,
The Alps are only shadows to the West,
That patch is India, the den of whales
A puddle—ecstasies on Everest!

And glided out beyond the atmosphere
Toward the moon. It trembled like a bell.
"Step right up, gentlemen!" Then sudden fear
Opened. I felt the precipice. I fell.

Down down like an umbrella I unfurled
My bones. I must have fallen for a week;
Then slowly and more slowly as the world
Unwrinkled, valley, plain and mountain peak.

And fell into the country of your eyes,
Since when I have lived comfortably here;
My thoughts are only clouds in summer skies,
And everything is perfect, calm and clear.

To the Western World

A siren sang, and Europe turned away
From the high castle and the shepherd's crook.
Three caravels went sailing to Cathay
On the strange ocean, and the captains shook
Their banners out across the Mexique Bay.

And in our early days we did the same.
Remembering our fathers in their wreck
We crossed the sea from Palos where they came
And saw, enormous to the little deck,
A shore in silence waiting for a name.

The treasures of Cathay were never found.
In this America, this wilderness
Where the axe echoes with a lonely sound,
The generations labor to possess
And grave by grave we civilize the ground.

Hot Night on Water Street

A hot midsummer night on Water Street—
The boys in jeans were combing their blond hair,
Watching the girls go by on tired feet;
And an old woman with a witch's stare
Cried "Praise the Lord!" She vanished on a bus
With hissing air brakes, like an incubus.

Three hardware stores, a barbershop, a bar,
A movie playing Westerns—where I went
To see a dream of horses called *The Star*. . . .
Some day, when this uncertain continent
Is marble, and men ask what was the good
We lived by, dust may whisper "Hollywood."

Then back along the river bank on foot
By moonlight. . . . On the West Virginia side
An owlish train began to huff and hoot;
It seemed to know of something that had died.
I didn't linger—sometimes when I travel
I think I'm being followed by the Devil.

At the newsstand in the lobby, a cigar
Was talkative: "Since I've been in this town
I've seen one likely woman, and a car
As she was crossing Main Street knocked her down."
I was a stranger here myself, I said,
And bought the *New York Times,* and went to bed.

The Boarder

The time is after dinner. Cigarettes
       Glow on the lawn;
Glasses begin to tinkle; TV sets
       Have been turned on.

The moon is brimming like a glass of beer
       Above the town,
And love keeps her appointments—"Harry's here!"
       "I'll be right down."

But the pale stranger in the furnished room
       Lies on his back
Looking at paper roses, how they bloom,
       And ceilings crack.

Orpheus in America

Here are your meadows, Love, as wide as heaven,
Green spirits, leaves
And winds, your ministers!

Item: a ship, that on the outer shoals
Lies broken. Item: thirty-seven souls,
Or rather, thirty-seven kinds of fever.
Item: three Indians, chained leg to leg.
Item: my lute.

This is the New England—rocks and brush
Where none may live but only tigers, parrots,
And mute imagining—
America, a desert with a name.

America begins antiquity.
Confronted with pure space, my Arcady
Has turned to stone.
Rome becomes Rome; Greece, Greece; the cottages
Collapse in ruin.

It darkens like a lapse of memory.
Here are no palaces, but lifted stone,
The pyramids of Egypt, stelcs
Of Ur. Columns that death has set
At the entrance to his kingdom.

II

This gazing freedom is the basilisk.
O for a mirror!
The melancholy of the possible
Unmeasures me.

Let music then begin. And let the air
Be passing sweet,
Music that scarcely wakes

The serpent in her trance
And leads the lion out into the dance.
And let the trees be moved,
And may the forest dance.

Then shall intelligence and grace
Join hands and sing: Goodbye to Arcady!
Another world is here, a greener Thrace!
Here are your meadows, Love, as wide as heaven,
Green spirits, leaves
And winds, your ministers,
In this America, this other, happy place.

An American in the Thieves' Market

In Italy the dead have all the passion.
They still reverberate among the broken
Columns and stones. And in comparison
    The living seem
Content, in the light-garlanded piazza,
To stare at beauty, strolling with no aim
Between the silly fountains and the dim
    Forgetful stream.

If I were an Italian, I'd pinch
Life on the thigh—*"Buon giorno!"* with a smile.
This is my business day: the offered bribe,
    Which I decline,
Then pocket—putting something in the glove
Of the police. At noon, enough of this.
And my old age is gazing, with my mistress,
    Cigars and wine.

But I am American, and bargain
In the Thieves' Market, where the junk of culture
Lies in the dust—clay shards, perhaps Etruscan,
    And wedding rings. . . .
My father's ghost is ticking in a watch,
My mother's, weeping in the antique bed,
And, in a pile of swords, my cousins shed
    The tears of things.

The Runner

This is the story of a soldier of the 101st Airborne Division of the Army of the United States.

The Runner is fiction; the episodes and characters are imaginary. But the fiction is based on the following history.

On September 17, 1944, parachute and glider infantry of the First British Airborne Division, the American 82nd and 101st Airborne Divisions, and a Polish brigade, descended in eastern Holland, at Eindhoven, Grave, Nijmegen and Arnhem. Their object was to make a bridgehead across the Lower Rhine at Arnhem. The British Second Army would join them and advance from Arnhem into the plains of northern Germany.

At Arnhem the British airborne troops were attacked by enemy units in overwhelming strength, and forced back across the river. The more fortunate Americans defended a corridor from Eindhoven to Nijmegen. The fighting, bitter at first, settled into a stalemate, and, with the coming of the rainy season, petered out entirely.

In mid-November the 82nd and 101st were drawn back to Rheims, to re-equip and get the drizzle out of their bones.

On December 17, they were alerted for combat. A German attack was developing in Belgium. The divisions were hurried by truck into the Ardennes, and on the night of December 19, the 101st were digging in around Bastogne.

I am most grateful to Mr. Donald Hall, who encouraged me to begin and to complete this story.

I

"And the condemned man ate a hearty meal,"
The runner said. He took his mess kit over
To the garbage can. He scraped his mess kit out,
Then dipped it in the can of soapy water,
And swished it in the can of clean, hot water,
And came back to his place.

The company
Was spread along one edge of the airfield,
Finishing lunch. Those with the appetite
Were going through the chow line once again.
They looked all pockets, pockets and baggy pants.
They held their mess kits out to the sweating cooks,
Who filled them up; then bore their precious load
Apart.

     The runner felt in his breast pocket
For cigarettes. He lit one and inhaled.
Leaning back on his pack, his feet sprawled out,
He stared at the ranks of gliders and tow planes
And said, "I wonder if . . ."

               "Agh!" said a voice,
"Why don't you dry up, Dodd!"

              He looked around
And met the eyes of Kass, the radioman,
Glaring beneath the rim of his steel helmet.

"What?" said the runner.

           "Who needs your remarks?
First, the condemned men eat a hearty meal,
And then you wonder . . ."

           "When we're coming back."

"What's it to you?"

          The runner didn't answer.
Sometimes it seemed that anything he said
Rubbed someone the wrong way. He'd only meant
He hoped the outfit would come back to England.
He liked the village where they had been quartered,
And London, where he'd gone on two-day passes.
He liked the pubs, the mugs of mild-and-bitter,
And country lanes. Some day, when they came back,

He'd go off on his own. Rent a bicycle.
He'd see some of the country by himself.
And if he got to London . . .

With a roar
An engine started. Other engines followed.
A gale from the propellers swept around him.

"Fall in!" said the First Sergeant.

Dodd got up
And hoisted on his pack.

"Get a move on!"

That's how it was: you always had to wait,
And then you had to hurry. He closed his belt,
And slung his rifle over his right shoulder.
The section formed.

"Where's Wheeler?" said the sergeant.
And here came Wheeler at a run. "You, Wheeler . . ."
The sergeant followed him with imprecations
As Wheeler ducked in place at Dodd's right hand.
Out of the side of his mouth: "Look what I got,"
Said Wheeler, and he showed in his clenched fist
A bundle of the new invasion money.
"Over in F Company," he whispered.
"The dice was really hot."

"Ten-*hut!* For-*ard*
Arch!" said the sergeant, and they started off
Across the concrete runway. It seemed long.
Dodd's mouth was dry; his legs were weak. At last
They came up to the glider, their box kite—
High wings and rudder, little wheels that hardly
Lifted it off the ground—a canvas coffin.
Ungainly as a duck, it wouldn't fly
Unless it had to.

5 4

Through the open door
Under the wing, they climbed up one by one,
Toppling with their burdens. Found their seats.
And sat in two rows, looking at each other.
Dodd fastened his safety belt and clasped his gun
Between his knees. The Captain entered last.
They waited. The glider trembled in the blast
Of wind from the tow plane. The pilots entered,
Leaping up lightly, and made their way forward
To the controls.

          The runner could see nothing
Beyond the glider's high, transparent nose;
But now, he thought, the tow plane would be turning
Into the wind. Two men would run the cable
Back from the plane and hook it to the glider.
Then, with a louder blast of the propellers,
The plane would start to roll.

                  The glider jerked
Forward, and rolled, creaking, and gathered speed.
The bumping stopped, and with a sudden lightness
They were air-borne. Constricted where he sat,
Dodd prayed to nothing in particular:
Let the rope hold; no current whirl us down
Smashing on concrete.

             They were well away.
He stared at the slender pilots in their pinks
And sporty caps and glasses; at their hands
On the half-wheel. His life was in those hands.
He thought of shell bursts, the green canvas torn,
Men writhing in their belts, the pilots' hands
Fallen from the controls, a sickening drop.
And then he thought of fields with pointed stakes
That would shear through the sides. Of plunging out
Into machine-gun fire.

                        "We're almost there,"
The next man said.

                    The pilots were peering down.
One nodded, and the other raised his hand
And grasped the lever that released the cable,
And pulled it down.

                      The glider soared, then fell
Slanting away. The wing rose up again.
They glided down on silence and the wind.

The fields were rushing at them, tilted steep.
Dodd braced himself. The glider leveled, lightly
Bumped on the ground, and rolled to a dead stop.

The door was open. They were climbing through.
And now were standing in an open field
Flat as a pancake. Gliders strewed the scene.
Others were skimming down; and still the sky
Was filled with gliders.

                  From their lifted bows
The gliders were disgorging jeeps and cannon.
Riflemen formed their files and marched away.
Dodd's section took its place in the company.
The Captain raised his arm; he swept it down,
And they were marching.

                  On the bright horizon
A windmill stood. The land was crossed with dykes.
It looked like a Dutch painting. To their left
A wood began. They marched in that direction.

The day was hot, and Dodd began to sweat.
Then to his ears came the familiar sound
Of guns, the battle-roll, continuous.
Then all his other days were like a dream.

This was reality: the heat, the load
Strapping his shoulders, and the sound of guns.

The war, after Normandy, had seemed remote.
He had been there; his courage had been proved
To his own satisfaction. He had listened
To talk about the fighting, and he'd talked
And lost the sense of truth. He had forgotten
The smell of apples and the fear of death.
Now he remembered. And it seemed unjust
That he should be required to survive
Again. The sound increased. The battleground
Looked ominous. Visions of a huge mistake
Struck at his heart.

III

The company was entering the woods.

"Dodd," said the sergeant, "take this message up
To Lieutenant Farr."

                            He stepped out of the file
And hastened to the front. The lead platoon
Was walking slowly, with the scouts ahead.
He gave the message.

                            "Right," said the lieutenant.
The runner started back. As he went by
Faces stared into his inquiringly.
He seemed possessed of an important secret.

Shots went off behind him. He crouched and swung
Out of the path, and lay in the scrub, face down.
The firing stopped. A voice was calling "Medic!"

Fisher, a sergeant of the third platoon,
Came up the path, bent low. He shook Dodd's shoulder:
"Who's doing all the shooting?"

        "I don't know,"
Dodd said. The sergeant, with a grim expression,
Stared at him, and went on.

        The runner waited.
Why didn't they get it over with!

        "Move out!"

He got to his feet. The path filled up with men.
He made his way back, past the sweating faces
Now streaked with dust. He fell in with his section,
Turned round, and traveled up the path again
He'd just traversed.

       The files ahead were parting.
The men looked down, as into a precipice.
There was a body lying in the way.
It was Santelli, of the first platoon.
Dodd had just seen him going out in front;
He walked like a dancer, with a short, neat step,
Rifle held crosswise.

       He lay huddled up
On his left side; his helmet had rolled off;
His head was seeping blood out in the dirt.

The files ahead were lagging; then they hurried.
"Keep your intervals!" the Captain shouted.
They hated him together.

      At the break
They sprawled out of the path, in the underbrush.
Santelli's death had made them strangely silent.
Their helmets bowed their heads down on their chests.
Under the distant thudding of the guns,
The weight of all their burdens and the sky,
They couldn't speak, or stir themselves, or lift
A cigarette.

5 8

Dodd thought about Santelli.
One of the afternoons it seemed forever
All they would do was practice for the war
With marches, tactics and map exercises,
He lay beneath the wall of an English garden,
Sucking a stalk of grass, and watched the clouds,
And far above the clouds, a fleet of bombers
Trailing long plumes of white across the blue.
Close by, Santelli sat, paring his nails
With a pocketknife.

                "Hey, runner-boy," he said
In the familiar and sneering tone
That Dodd despised. "What're we doin, hey?
You've been to college, right?" His little eyes
Were sharp with mockery—a little man
Of pocketknives and combs. "You ought to know.
What's it all about?"

        IV

A plane flew glittering out of the sun—
A Thunderbolt. It swooped and disappeared
Behind a screen of trees. Then a staccato
Sound began. Machine guns. The plane rose
And flew away. They watched it till it vanished.

"On your feet," the sergeant said.

                "My aching back!"
Someone said; but the gripe lacked conviction.
They stood and crumbled out their cigarettes,
And rolled the paper into little balls,
As though they'd like to keep the battlefield
Clean as a barracks.

            As Dodd marched, the weight
Sawed at his shoulders: pack and ammunition,
Gas mask and trench tool, bayonet, grenades.

He plodded with clenched jaws, his eyes cast down
On the dusty path, the heels moving ahead.
He stayed, it seemed, in a fixed position;
It was the scene that moved.

                    The path reeled in
Another corpse. It came to him boot-first:
A German soldier on his back, spread-eagle,
A big, fresh-blooded, blond, jack-booted man
In dusty gray. Stepping around the fingers,
Around the bucket helmet, Dodd stared down.
A fly lit on the teeth. He looked away
And to the front, where other attitudes
Of death were waiting. He assumed them all,
One by one, in his imagination,
In order to prevent them.

                    Small-arms fire
Was crackling through the wood. Platoons spread out
In arrow-shaped formations.

                    "Dig in!"

                              He dug.
The shovel sank in sand; he hacked at roots.
Overhead, shells were whispering, and smoke
Came drifting back.

                    Two planes went whistling over.
Typhoons. They darted searching on the front.
They dived, and from their wings plunged rockets down
In smoking streaks. The ground shook with concussions.

"We're moving out!"

                    Dodd climbed out of the hole
That he had dug. The company moved in silence
Through the burning wood.

V

Beyond the wood there stretched an open road.
They filed out on it. In a field of hay
A plane perched on its nose, a Messerschmidt,
The black cross glaring.

                Houses stood here and there.
In front of one, a mattress had been laid,
And on the mattress, a German officer.
He was puffed up with air like a balloon,
Belly and limbs swelling as if to split
His uniform. The grass was stuck with feathers.

Night was falling; the light had left the fields.
The road approached a village. At the entrance
A German half-track had been blown apart,
Its mustard-yellow metal torn and scorched;
Out of it spilled the crew, burned black as rubber.
The street, as they passed through, was strewn with dead,
A presentation of boot soles and teeth,
Letters, cigars, the contents of their lives.

The cannonading was more loud, and flashes
Lit the darkening sky. A company
Of paratroopers passed them, coming back
With somber faces.

VI

Night. And the fields were still. The cannonade
Was flickering and grumbling through the sky.
Red flashes lined the clouds. No breath of wind
Was moving. In the holes that they had dug
The tired troops were sleeping on their arms.

"Dodd, get up!"

           He struggled out of his bag.

The First Sergeant leaned over: "Take this message
Back to Battalion."

          Dodd took the paper,
His helmet and his M-1, and set off,
Still half asleep.

          Darkness without a moon
Surrounded him. He made his lonely way
Over a road that skirted trees and dykes.
The guns were rumbling; shells went fluttering over;
Machine-gun tracers sparkled distantly.
A flare popped in the sky and glimmered down;
He waited in the shadow of a tree
Till it went out. And took the road again.

Battalion were in a farmhouse. The roof line
Loomed in front of him, and a guard called: "Halt!
Who's there?"

          The runner spoke the password:
"Kansas!" and was admitted by the guard
Into the farmyard. There he gave his message
To a tech sergeant; sat down on a bench,
And waited, looking at the pulsing sky.

"Runner!"

          He answered.

              "Take this message back."

That was his job. Now all I need, he thought,
Is one of those Philip Morris uniforms
The bell boys wear.

          The road was long and dark.
And it was weird to be alone in Holland
At midnight on this road. As he went on
He felt he had no weight. The landscape seemed
To have more things to think of than his journey.

These errands gave him little satisfaction.
Some men might think he led the life of Riley,
Safe and warm and dry, around Headquarters.
A man could be a runner all his life
And never be shot at. That's what they thought.
But how about the shelling? He'd been shelled
As much as anyone. And back in France,
At Carentan, he had been shot at—plenty!
It wasn't his fault he never had a chance
To fire back. Now, right here on this road,
He might be killed by accident. But still,
That wouldn't be the same as being brave.
He had no chance to be thought so, no part
In the society of riflemen.
So, as he went, he reasoned with himself.

VII

Next day the company went up on line
Near Veghel. They were digging round a church,
In the cemetery, and were just knee-deep
When hell broke loose.

                      The screaming and flat crack
Of eighty-eights.

           Air bursts.

                 The metal slashed
The trees and ricocheted. Bit in the ground.

The runner on his belly lay contracting
Under the edge of metal. From a tree
A yard away, leaves flew.

                A voice cried "Medic!"

His belly and his buttocks clenched each time
A shell came in. And they kept coming in.
He felt a sting between his shoulder blades.

I'm wounded! he thought, with a rush of joy.

"Dodd!" someone called.

          He went on hands and knees
Toward the voice.

        "Over here," it urged him.

It was his sergeant, with a dozen cases
Of mortar shells.

       "Take them up to the mortars,"
The sergeant said. "They're out of ammunition."

He took two cases, one beneath each arm,
And ran off, dodging among the trees and graves.
He found the mortars and came running back
To get another load. The crack and hum
Of the artillery was all around him.
He felt the sting of the place where he'd been hit.
He knew that he was brave.

         On the last trip,
Kneeling above a mortar, as he lowered
The cases gently, one of the mortar crew
Said, "You're a good man, Dodd."

         That night he lay
Smiling, without a care, beneath the sky.
He had done all that could be expected.

VIII

October, and the sky was turning gray.
The battle-line had settled. Every night
The bombers flew, going to Germany
At a great height. And back the other way
The V-1's came. The soldiers in their holes
Heard them droning and saw the rhythmic flames
Carrying woe to Antwerp and to England.

They dozed or watched. Then it began to rain,
And always rained. It seemed they were never dry.
Winter was in the air. Paths turned to mud.
By day and night the shells came shrieking in;
They got so they could tell a dying fall
And pay the rest no mind. They lived with mud.
They cooked and ate their rations in the can,
And tried to dry their socks between two rains.
Cold and sullen, under a raincoat roof,
They shivered in their holes.

                        One moonlit night
Dodd was returning on his way alone.
There was a wind; the haunted shadows stirred,
And rainpools glimmered in the moonlit fields.

There was a field the runner loathed to cross.
A place of horrors. Here, on the first day,
There'd been fierce charges, combats at close range,
And the dead were mixed as they had fallen.
Here crouched the German soldier with his *schmeisser*
Close to the parachutist in his rage—
Putrid things, never to be forgotten.
The field was swelling, shining with an aura
Of pale corruption.

               To avoid it, Dodd
Went by another path he did not know,
Leading, it seemed, back to the company.
But in a while a fearful premonition
Stopped him. In a shadow, cold with dread,
He stood listening. The branches stirred,
And all at once there was a clash of arms,
The sound of footsteps. Stealthily he turned
To slip away.

           "*Wer geht da?*"

                 He ran.

He plunged into the darkness, blind with panic.
A storm of shots erupted at his back.
Brambles tore at his legs. He climbed a bank,
Clawing, and stumbled down the other side.
Then, as he ran, he shouted out the password:
"Ohio!" like a dog drenched with hot water.
His rifle fell. He left it where it was.
"Ohio!" He collided with a branch
And staggered. At his back the storm increased.
Red tracers streaked the air. Across a ditch
He leaped. And ran across the road beyond.
A hole was in his way; he cleared it with
A stride, and the dark figure starting up
Out of the hole. He kept on running, shouting
"Ohio!" A shape standing in the path
Snatched at him; he swerved out of its grasp.
There was a maze of holes. He stumbled, reeled,
And fell. His helmet flew off with a clang.

Feet were approaching. He lay still as death.

"It's Dodd," said a voice.

                  At last, he looked up
Into the faces of the third platoon.
Fisher. Others. They looked down in wonder.

IX

The regiment was bivouacked near Rheims
In tents on the bare plain. Wind-driven clouds
Streamed over, and the land in chilly streaks
Heaved like a sea. The wind hummed on the ropes
And whipped the tent flaps.

                  Dodd, stretched on his cot,
Could see and hear the third platoon at drill.
They turned to the flank and to the flank again;
They marched to the rear.

"Count cadence . . . cadence count!"
"Hup . . . two . . . three . . . four!" they answered on
    the wind.
The sun flashed from the slanting rifle butts.

The corporal shouted: "When I say Ohio,
To the rear march, and double-time like hell!"
There was a burst of laughter, then: "Ohio!
Run!" the corporal said, *"Hup* . . . two . . . three . . .
    four!
Halt! Now we'll try that movement once again.
When I give the word Ohio, turn around
And double-time as if your name is Dodd.
Make it look good. All right now—forward *'arch!*
Ohio!"

    Dodd rolled over on his face.
He saw himself once more before the Captain:
"Screaming the password . . . throwing away your gun . . .
Keep out of my sight, Dodd. You make me sick."

And then, the jokes, from reveille to sleep:
"That's Ohio, one of the Midwest boys."
Replacements would be sent to see Ohio
To draw their running shoes. "I'm from Cleveland,"
One of them told him. "What part are you from?"

He turned upon his back. Right overhead
His jacket hung, with regimental ribbons,
The bronze star, and his shameful purple heart.
He stared at it. If he could only sleep
The time between, until the sergeant came
To put him on another hard detail!
That was his punishment: to dig latrines,
Pick cigarette butts up, scrub greasy pots—
Or to do nothing for a live-long day
But think and try to read, in a cold tent.

When the men came in, they would ignore him—

"You going in to town?"

"You said it, man!"

Polishing up their paratrooper boots
Until the toes reflected a lit match;
Blousing the trousers in their boot-tops; brushing
Their jackets; tucking ties between two buttons;
Cocking their caps—

"Let's go!"

He fell asleep,
And dreamed that he was climbing. On the crest
A dummy stood, with stiff, ballooning arms
And painted face, in Prussian uniform.
He reached the arms and swung them. It went "B-r-r-r-m!"
Like a machine gun. "B-r-r-r-m!" the sound came out
The dummy's painted lips and barrel belly.
Then he was walking over a green field.
It was a country he had never seen,
With haystacks, a warm wind, and distant barns.
Shadows were walking with him, and a voice
Spoke with the measure of a travelogue:
"Vingtième Division . . . fifty per cent . . ."
Another voice inquired: "Casualties?"
"No," said the first voice, "all of them are dead."
And it continued: "Douzième Infanterie . . .
Fifty per cent . . ." As the first voice was speaking,
Over the field, as on a movie screen,
Hands were imposed; they held a scarlet cloth
And folded it. "René de Gaumartin,"
The voice continued, "Cardinal of France."
Again the hands were folding a red robe.
"Marcel Gaumartin, Cardinal of France."
And as the voice and the pale hands continued
Their meditative play, Dodd came upon

A girl in black. She had fair hair and skin,
Plain features, almost ugly, but her eyes
Were large, they shot out tender rays of light.
The voice said, "Mademoiselle de Maintenon."
In his dream, Dodd laughed. *De Maintenon!* She said,
In a voice remote with sadness, "Yes," and smiled,
"I try not to think of them too much."

       He woke,
And his heart was light. It was a vision,
He thought. What does it mean? What eyes she had!
That field, with the wind blowing, and the clouds!
And yet, it was absurd. The words were nonsense.

He went out of his tent.

     The third platoon
Were sitting down, taking a smoking break.
"Ohio!" someone shouted. "Where you running?"

He walked the other way, toward a rise
With trees, the only trees in all the plain,
Leaving the tents behind.

      He climbed the slope
And sat beneath a tree. On the horizon
Rheims, with the cathedral, like a ship
Traveled the plain. Clouds were streaming over
The spire; their swift shadows ran like waves.
He lit a cigarette. Then, near at hand,
He saw the earth was trenched. A long depression,
No more than a foot deep, with rotten posts
And scraps of wire, wound across the slope.
He stood, and walked along it. The earth gave
Under his boots. He picked up a small scrap
Of wire, and it crumbled. He surmised
This was a trench dug in the first Great War.
Who knew? Perhaps an older war than that.
He faced the East, to Germany and Russia.

Shadows were standing with him. It was cold.
They watched, wrapped in old overcoats, forgotten.
They stamped their feet. The whole world was deserted
Except for them; there was nobody left.
On the imagined parapet, a cross
Howled in the wind; and there were photographs
Of girls and children; bunches of cut flowers.
Then, on the pitted, gaunt escarp, the night,
The melancholy night, swept with grandeur.
Far in the dark, star-shells were blossoming.
They stamped their feet. It was too cold. Too much
To expect of them. Their boots sank in the mud.
Their veins seemed ice; their jaws creaked with the cold.
They spoke; their words were carried on the wind,
Mingled, and lost.

      But now, an actual sound
Arrived distinctly. When he turned to look,
The camp was stirring; men ran to and fro.
He saw the third platoon halt in their drill,
Fall out, and run toward their tents. He moved;
He ground his cigarette out underfoot,
And hastened down the slope.

        "Where have you been?"
Said the First Sergeant.

       "I've been for a walk.
What's going on?"

       "Full field. Ready to move
In half an hour."

      Dodd's tent was in confusion.
The men were cramming rations in their packs,
Rolling their sleeping bags, cleaning their weapons.
He labored with stiff fingers.

       Trucks drew up
Outside.

"Get a move on!" a corporal shouted.

Dodd hitched on his pack.

           The company
Fell in and shuffled, straightening their ranks,
Eyes to the right.

          "Let's go!"

             Dodd took his place
In the line of olive-drab, the overcoats,
Helmets, packs, the gloved hands holding weapons.
The roll was called; he answered to his name.

They marched up to the trucks.

              "Mount up!"

                 He climbed
Into the truck, and was packed in. The gate
Clanged shut behind him.

       x
Day turned to dusk; the truck went jolting on;
The wind was drumming on the canvas hood
And prying coldly down the runner's back.
Dusk turned to evening, and the trucks behind
Were hidden. He dozed off. Monotony
Had numbed his senses like an anesthetic.
When the gears shifted he would nearly wake.
Sometimes the truck would stop for no clear reason,
And faces, blinking in their woolen caps,
Lifted and muttered; someone tried to stretch,
And this set off a ripple of complaints.
Then the truck moved again.

             Once they dismounted,
And Dodd saw that the road wound through a forest.
There was a hill on one side; on the other,

The trees descended into a ravine.
Against that bank, a group of people stood:
Women and children dressed in country black,
With kerchiefs round their heads, and an old man
Close to a cart. The cart was piled with things:
A mattress, pots and pans. They stood in silence
Watching the soldiers. Then the trucks reloaded,
And the onlookers vanished.

      They were driving
More slowly now. The men were all awake.
Another stop. Again the tail-gate opened,
And they dismounted.

     This, then, was the place.
Colliding in the dark, they formed platoons,
And marched away.

    A signpost read *Bastogne*.
They marched through a dark village with locked doors,
And were led off the road, into the woods.
The path was very dark, the march confused,
With frequent halts.

     They halted in one place
Endlessly; they reclined, propped on their packs.
His helmet dragged Dodd's head back on his neck;
His feet got cold; under his woolen shirt
The sweat was trickling, then began to chill.

Then they were roused, pressed on without a pause,
Till, on a ridge commanding a black slope,
They halted. And the order came: "Dig in!"

Dodd unhitched his pack, laid it on the ground,
And leaned his rifle on it. From his belt
He took his trench-tool out, and opened it.
He stuck the shovel blade into the ground
And levered it. He'd barely circumscribed

A foxhole, when a cold chill touched his cheek—
Snow!

       That's all we needed, the runner said
To the malignant sky.

           From branch to branch
Snow glimmered down and speckled the dim ground.
Dodd dragged a fallen branch across his hole
And made a roof.

          "Pack up," the sergeant said.
"We're moving out."

          God help them, they were led
By officers and morons, who had orders
For wearing leather out and breaking spades,
To give employment to the men at home
Who, on this freezing night, were warm in bed
With soldiers' wives!

          Having said so, they walked
On in the stumbling dark, till once again
They halted, in a place just like the first.

"Dig in!"

      And it was useless, but they dug
With the energy of a supreme contempt
Marvelous holes—each clammy wedge of earth
An accusation flung in heaven's face.

Then, like a sound engendered by their mood,
An angry muttering rose on the night.
It faded, and again came to their ears—
The sound of guns.

         At last, Dodd's hole was finished.
He lowered himself, rolled out his sleeping bag,
And pushed into it. Flickerings of light

Twitched overhead; the guns were coming closer.
Here, it was still. The snow came drifting down.

"Dodd, you're on guard."

He climbed out of his hole.

"There, by the trees."

He walked across the snow,
And as he went he looked around, astonished—
The sky was lit with spots of burning red
In a great circle.

As he stood on guard,
Surveying the black slope, the distant fires,
A man approached. Dodd challenged him. He spoke
The password, and came slogging through the trees.
A runner from Battalion. Brushing snow
Out of his neck, he asked for the C. P.
Dodd pointed: "Over there. Close to the barn.
What's happening now?"

"We're up a creek, that's what!
They're coming—panzers from the Russian front,
Under Von Runstedt. Panzers and SS.
I was just talking to a man who said
The line at St. Vith has been overrun
By tanks. It was a total massacre.
They're dropping paratroopers too," he said,
And turned away. He paused again to add:
"Everyone else is pulling out but us,"
And trudged away, leaving Dodd to his thoughts.

XI

The night was long. And day seemed less to rise
Than darkness to withdraw. Dodd, in his hole,
Could hear the fire of small arms, that seems
More threatening to the solitary man
Than does artillery.

                    One hole away
A helmet like a turtle shell was stirring.
A puffy face with whiskers turned around;
It was the mailman, Lopez. He arranged
Twigs on the snow. On these, his drinking mug.
He struck a match, applied it to the twigs,
And nursed the flame with cupped hands, bending over.

Under the hanging sky, congealed with clouds,
Fog trailed and clung to the earth; and the Ardennes,
The spectral firs, their branches cloaked with snow,
Stood stark against the foggy atmosphere.

Dodd stamped his feet. He stooped, and from his pack
Took a K-ration box. He tore it open,
Shook out the can of egg, the pack of biscuits,
The packet of coffee. He removed a glove
And with that hand put snow into his mug.
Poured coffee in, and mixed it with his spoon.
He scooped a hollow in the snow, and piled
Some twigs in it, and strips of the ration box.
And then put the mug on, and lit the pile.

Voices came floating up—loud gutturals;
A whine and clanking of machinery.
He picked his gun up.

                    At the foot of the slope
The trees were shaking, parting. There emerged
A cannon barrel with a muzzle-brake.
It slid out like a snake's head, slowly swinging.
It paused. A flash of light came from its head;
A thunderclap exploded to Dodd's left;
Metal whanged on the slope, a spume of black
Hung in the air.

                    Then, endlessly it seemed,
The barrel slid out. With a thrash of branches
A tank appeared. It lurched, seemed to consider,

And then came on, at an appalling rate.
The engine whined; the tracks jingled and squeaked.
And imperceptibly, out of the trees
Stood men, like apparitions of the snow.

And now it was a swarm of walking men
In field gray and in white, with capes and hoods.

Dodd placed his elbows on the snow, took aim—
There was another thunderclap. He ducked
And came upright again. To left and right
Rifles were firing. Hastily he pointed
The muzzle at a running, hooded shape,
And pressed the trigger. As in a nightmare
Nothing happened. A bullet cracked by his head.
The safety catch was on. He pressed it forward,
And aimed the gun again, and squeezed the trigger.
The butt kicked in his shoulder, the brass jumped
Into the snow.

           The tank was growing large.
The cannon flashed. Machine-gun tracers curved
Toward it, and played sparkling on the steel.
Still it came on, glittering in return
From its machine guns. Then, a crashing flame
Struck it, leaving a trail of smoke in air.
The tank shuddered. It slewed broadside around.
Inside the plates, as on an anvil, hammers
Were laboring. It trembled with explosions,
And smoke poured out of it.

              The slope was still,
Sprawling with hooded figures—and the rest
Gone back into the trees. Then there began
The sound of the wounded.

           Dodd stood up
And looked around. In the next hole, a helmet
Moved cautiously.

"Lopez," he inquired,
"Are you all right?"

"Jesus!" the mailman said.

With a shaking hand, Dodd felt for cigarettes.
He breathed tobacco deep into his lungs.
On the twigs where he had left it balanced
His mug was hissing and—he held it—warm.

XII

Sometimes the snow came drifting down again.
And when it ceased, eddies and gusts of wind
Would lift it in long skirts that swept across
The dead. It packed into the stiffened folds
Of clothing. When night fell, a freezing wind
Encased the tree-trunks in bright sheaths of ice
And hung bright icicles on every branch,
And clamped the dead in rigid attitudes.

A shell came whistling down. The runner clenched
His fists. It crashed. Another shell came in.
The crashes jarred the ground. Then, from the rear,
A battery replied; shells fluttered back.

"Dodd!"

He unzipped his bag, put on his helmet,
And stood.

"Where are you?"

It was the First Sergeant.

"Here," the runner answered.

"Take this message
Back to Battalion. Are you listening?"

"Yes," he said.

"To Colonel Jesserman.
The Captain says we need a fifty-seven
Or tank-destroyer. Tell him that it's urgent.
Now you repeat the message."

                              Dodd did so.
He slung his rifle over his right shoulder
And climbed out of his hole.

                              "Keep out of trouble,"
The sergeant said. "Don't stop for anything."
Dodd started to move off. The sergeant grasped
His arm: "Watch out! They may have got patrols
Between us and Battalion. Good luck!"

Dodd waved his hand, although it was too dark
For the other to see him. And set off
In what seemed to be the right direction.

Rome. December 2, 1957

Old Soldier

A dream of battle on a windy night
Has wakened him. The shadows move once more
With rumors of alarm. He sees the height
And helmet of his terror in the door.

The guns reverberate; a livid arc
From sky to sky lightens the windowpanes
And all his room. The clock ticks in the dark;
A cool wind stirs the curtains, and it rains.

He lies remembering: "That's how it was . . ."
And smiles, and drifts into a youthful sleep
Without a care. His life is all he has,
And that is given to the guards to keep.

The Bird

"Ich wünscht', ich wäre ein Vöglein,"
Sang Heinrich, "I would fly
Across the sea . . ." so sadly
It made his mother cry.

At night he played his zither,
By day worked in the mine.
His friend was Hans; together
The boys walked by the Rhine.

"Each day we're growing older,"
Hans said, "This is no life.
I wish I were a soldier!"
And snapped his pocketknife.

War came, and Hans was taken,
But Heinrich did not fight.
"Ich wünscht', ich wäre ein Vöglein,"
Sang Heinrich every night.

"Dear Heinrich," said the letter,
"I hope this finds you fine.
The war could not be better,
It's women, song and wine."

A letter came for Heinrich,
The same that he'd sent East
To Hans, his own handwriting
Returned, and marked *Deceased*.

*

"You'll never be a beauty,"
The doctor said, "You scamp!
We'll give you special duty—
A concentration camp."

And now the truck was nearing
The place. They passed a house;
A radio was blaring
The *Wiener Blut* of Strauss.

The banks were bright with flowers,
The birds sang in the wood;
There was a fence with towers
On which armed sentries stood.

They stopped. The men dismounted;
Heinrich got down—at last!
"That chimney," said the sergeant,
"That's where the Jews are gassed."

*

Each day he sorted clothing,
Skirt, trousers, boot and shoe,
Till he was filled with loathing
For every size of Jew.

"Come in! What is it, Private?"
"Please Sir, that vacancy . . .
I wonder, could I have it?"
"Your papers! Let me see . . .

"You're steady and you're sober . . .
But have you learned to kill?"
Said Heinrich, "No, *Herr Ober-
Leutnant,* but I will!"

"The Reich can use your spirit.
Report to Unit Four.
Here is an arm-band—wear it!
Dismissed! Don't slam the door."

*

"Ich wünscht', ich wäre ein Vöglein,"
Sang Heinrich, "I would fly . . ."
They knew that when they heard him
The next day they would die.

They stood in silence praying
At midnight when they heard
The zither softly playing,
The singing of the Bird.

He stared into the fire,
He sipped a glass of wine.
"Ich wünscht'," his voice rose higher,
"Ich wäre ein Vöglein . . ."

A dog howled in its kennel,
He thought of Hans and cried.
The stars looked down from heaven.
That day the children died.

*

"The Russian tanks are coming!"
The wind bore from the east
A cannonade, a drumming
Of small arms that increased.

Heinrich went to Headquarters.
He found the Colonel dead
With pictures of his daughters,
A pistol by his head.

He thought, his courage sinking,
"There's always the SS . . ."
He found the Major drinking
In a woman's party dress.

The prisoners were shaking
Their barracks. Heinrich heard
A sound of timber breaking,
A shout, "Where is the Bird?"

*

The Russian was completing
A seven-page report.
He wrote: "We still are beating
The woods . . ." then he stopped short.

A little bird was flitting
Outside, from tree to tree.
He turned where he was sitting
And watched it thoughtfully.

He pulled himself together,
And wrote: "We've left no stone
Unturned—but not a feather!
It seems the Bird has flown.

"Description? Half a dozen
Group snapshots, badly blurred;
And which is Emma's cousin
God knows, and which the Bird!

"He could be in the Western
Or in the Eastern Zone.
I'd welcome a suggestion
If anything is known."

*

"Ich wünscht', ich wäre ein Vöglein,"
Sings Heinrich, "I would fly
Across the sea," so sadly
It makes his children cry.

The Silent Generation

When Hitler was the Devil
He did as he had sworn
With such enthusiasm
That even, *donnerwetter,*
The Germans say, "Far better
Had he been never born!"

It was my generation
That put the Devil down
With great enthusiasm.
But now our occupation
Is gone. Our education
Is wasted on the town.

We lack enthusiasm.
Life seems a mystery;
It's like the play a lady
Told me about: "It's not . . .
It doesn't *have* a plot,"
She said, "it's history."

The Custom of the World

O, we loved long and happily, God knows!
The ocean danced, the green leaves tossed, the air
Was filled with petals, and pale Venus rose
When we began to kiss. Kisses brought care,
And closeness caused the taking off of clothes.
O, we loved long and happily, God knows!

"The watchdogs are asleep, the doormen doze. . . ."
We huddled in the corners of the stair,
And then we climbed it. What had we to lose?
What would we gain? The best way to compare
And quickest, was by taking off our clothes.
O, we loved long and happily, God knows!

Between us two a silent treason grows,
Our pleasures have been changed into despair.
Wild is the wind, from a cold country blows,
In which these tender blossoms disappear.
And did this come of taking off our clothes?
O, we loved long and happily, God knows!

Mistress, my song is drawing to a close.
Put on your rumpled skirt and comb your hair,
And when we meet again let us suppose
We never loved or ever naked were.
For though this nakedness was good, God knows,
The custom of the world is wearing clothes.

The Lover's Ghost

I fear the headless man
Whose military scars
Proclaim his merit.
And yet I fear a woman
More than the ghost of Mars,
A wounded spirit.

That look, all kindness lost,
Cold hands, as cold as stone,
A wanton gesture—
"What do you want, old ghost?
How long must I atone?"
So I addressed her.

"Did you not call?" she said,
"Goodbye, then! For I go
Where I am wanted."
Till dawn I tossed in bed
Wishing that I could know
Who else she haunted.

The Goodnight

He stood still by her bed
Watching his daughter breathe,
The dark and silver head,
The fingers curled beneath,
And thought: Though she may have
Intelligence and charm
And luck, they will not save
Her life from every harm.

The lives of children are
Dangerous to their parents
With fire, water, air,
And other accidents;
And some, for a child's sake,
Anticipating doom,
Empty the world to make
The world safe as a room.

Who could endure the pain
That was Laocoön's?
Twisting, he saw again
In the same coil his sons.
Plumed in his father's skill,
Young Icarus flew higher
Toward the sun, until
He fell in rings of fire.

A man who cannot stand
Children's perilous play,
With lifted voice and hand
Drives the children away.
Out of sight, out of reach,
The tumbling children pass;
He sits on an empty beach,
Holding an empty glass.

Who said that tenderness
Will turn the heart to stone?
May I endure her weakness
As I endure my own.
Better to say goodnight
To breathing flesh and blood
Each night as though the night
Were always only good.

AT THE END OF THE
OPEN ROAD

1963

In California

Here I am, troubling the dream coast
With my New York face,
Bearing among the realtors
And tennis-players my dark preoccupation.

There once was an epical clatter—
Voices and banjos, Tennessee, Ohio,
Rising like incense in the sight of heaven.
Today, there is an angel in the gate.

Lie back, Walt Whitman,
There, on the fabulous raft with the King and the Duke!
For the white row of the Marina
Faces the Rock. Turn round the wagons here.

Lie back! We cannot bear
The stars any more, those infinite spaces.
Let the realtors divide the mountain,
For they have already subdivided the valley.

Rectangular city blocks astonished
Herodotus in Babylon,
Cortez in Tenochtitlan,
And here's the same old city-planner, death.

We cannot turn or stay.
For though we sleep, and let the reins fall slack,
The great cloud-wagons move
Outward still, dreaming of a Pacific.

In the Suburbs

There's no way out.
You were born to waste your life.
You were born to this middleclass life

As others before you
Were born to walk in procession
To the temple, singing.

The Redwoods

Mountains are moving, rivers
are hurrying. But we
are still.

We have the thoughts of giants—
clouds, and at night the stars.

And we have names—guttural, grotesque—
Hamet, Og—names with no syllables.

And perish, one by one, our roots
gnawed by the mice. And fall.

And are too slow for death, and change
to stone. Or else too quick,

like candles in a fire. Giants
are lonely. We have waited long

for someone. By our waiting, surely
there must be someone at whose touch

our boughs would bend; and hands
to gather us; a spirit

to whom we are light as the hawthorn tree.
O if there is a poet

let him come now! We stand at the Pacific
like great unmarried girls,

turning in our heads the stars and clouds,
considering whom to please.

There Is

Look! From my window there's a view
of city streets
where only lives as dry as tortoises
can crawl—the Galapagos of desire.

There is the day of Negroes with red hair
and the day of insane women on the subway;
there is the day of the word Trieste
and the night of the blind man with the electric guitar.

But I have no profession. Like a spy
I read the papers—Situations Wanted.
Surely there is a secret
which, if I knew it, would change everything!

2

I have the poor man's nerve-tic, irony.
I see through the illusions of the age!
The bell tolls, and the hearse advances,
and the mourners follow, for my entertainment.

I tread the burning pavement,
the streets where drunkards stretch
like photographs of civil death
and trumpets strangle in electric shelves.

The mannequins stare at me scornfully.
I know they are pretending
all day to be in earnest.
And can it be that love is an illusion?

When darkness falls on the enormous street
the air is filled with Eros, whispering.
Eyes, mouths, contrive to meet
in silence, fearing they may be prevented.

3

O businessmen like ruins,
bankers who are Bastilles,
widows, sadder than the shores of lakes,
then you were happy, when you still could tremble!

But all night long my window
sheds tears of light.
I seek the word. The word is not forthcoming.
O syllables of light . . . O dark cathedral . . .

Summer Morning

There are whole blocks in New York
Where no one lives—
A district of small factories.
And there's a hotel; one morning

When I was there with a girl
We saw in the window opposite
Men and women working at their machines.
Now and then one looked up.

Toys, hardware—whatever they made,
It's been worn out.
I'm fifteen years older myself—
Bad years and good.

So I have spoiled my chances.
For what? Sheer laziness,
The thrill of an assignation,
My life that I hold in secret.

The Silent Lover

She sighs. What shall I say?
For beauty seems to grow
In silence, when the heart is faint and slow.

Sing, sing . . . How shall I sing?
In silent eyes, where clouds and islands gaze,
The waves bring Eros in.

I think the rustling of her clothes
Is like the sea, and she
A wild white bird,

And love is like the sighing of the sand.

Birch

Birch tree, you remind me
Of a room filled with breathing,
The sway and whisper of love.

She slips off her shoes;
Unzips her skirt; arms raised,
Unclasps an earring, and the other.

Just so the sallow trunk
Divides, and the branches
Are pale and smooth.

The Morning Light

In the morning light a line
Stretches forever. There my unlived life
Rises, and I resist,
Clinging to the steps of the throne.

Day lifts the darkness from the hills,
A bright blade cuts the reeds,
And my life, pitilessly demanding,
Rises forever in the morning light.

The Cradle Trap

A bell and rattle,
a smell of roses,
a leather Bible,
and angry voices . . .

They say, I love you.
They shout, You must!
The light is telling
terrible stories.

But night at the window
whispers, Never mind.
Be true, be true
to your own strange kind.

A Story about Chicken Soup

In my grandmother's house there was always chicken soup
And talk of the old country—mud and boards,
Poverty,
The snow falling down the necks of lovers.

Now and then, out of her savings
She sent them a dowry. Imagine
The rice-powdered faces!
And the smell of the bride, like chicken soup.

But the Germans killed them.
I know it's in bad taste to say it,
But it's true. The Germans killed them all.

*

In the ruins of Berchtesgaden
A child with yellow hair
Ran out of a doorway.

A German girl-child—
Cuckoo, all skin and bones—
Not even enough to make chicken soup.
She sat by the stream and smiled.

Then as we splashed in the sun
She laughed at us.
We had killed her mechanical brothers,
So we forgave her.

*

The sun is shining.
The shadows of the lovers have disappeared.
They are all eyes; they have some demand on me—
They want me to be more serious than I want to be.

They want me to stick in their mudhole
Where no one is elegant.
They want me to wear old clothes,
They want me to be poor, to sleep in a room with many others—

Not to walk in the painted sunshine
To a summer house,
But to live in the tragic world forever.

The Troika

Troika, troika! The snow moon
whirls through the forest.

Where lamplight like a knife
gleams through a door, I see two graybeards bending.
They're playing chess, it seems. And then one rises
and stands in silence. Does he hear me passing?

Troika, troika! In the moonlight
his spirit hears my spirit passing.

I whip the horses on. The houses vanish.
The moon looks over fields
littered with debris. And there in trenches
the guardsmen stand, wind fluttering their rags.

And there were darker fields without a moon.
I walk across a field, bound on an errand.
The errand's forgotten—something depended on it.
A nightmare! I have lost my father's horses!

And then a white bird rises
and goes before me, hopping through the forest.

I held the bird—it vanished with a cry,
and on a branch a girl sat sideways, combing
her long black hair. The dew
shone on her lips; her breasts were white as roses.

Troika, troika! Three white horses,
a whip of silver, and my father's sleigh . . .

When morning breaks, the sea
gleams through the branches,
and the white bird, enchanted,
is flying through the world, across the sea.

Moving the Walls

The Prince of Monaco
Was sick of English ladies.

The Prince had a yacht
And her name was *Hirondelle*.
She was cousin to the yacht of the Kaiser
And niece to the yacht of the Tsar.

And the Prince was interested in the sea—
That is, oceanography.
So he furnished the yacht with instruments
And with instruments of brass,
Burners and sinks and instruments
Of the most delicate glass.

There was also a whaleboat
And a whole crew of harpooners.
There was a helmet and suit of armor
For the wars of the ocean floor.

The *Hirondelle* trembled like a fern,
And the crew stood at attention,
And they piped the Captain aboard.

2

Cloud-sailed, the *Hirondelle*
Pursued the horizon.
At night she skimmed
The phosphorescent surges.

And now they are on the Pacific,
The bottomless sea.
And out of the deep they have drawn
The whale, Leviathan, with a hook.
They have captured the giant squid
That has ten arms, claws like a cat's, a beak like a parrot's,
And a large malevolent eye.

They stepped from the whaleboat onto shoals,
The crests of sunken mountains.
In nets they gathered
Plankton and weeds and crabs that looked astonished.

And there were nights, O Prince,
When you stretched your hands and feet
In the leaves of the pomegranate tree!

And all went into the log.
The various sea trophies
Were written down in the log.
The darkening sky, the storm,
And tranquil days—
All, all went into the log.

3

The Prince returned—a hero of sorts.
He returned to his former life,
To the lights of the Grand Hotel
And the Russian ladies with their eternal cigarettes.

Then he built a museum.
The wheel of the *Hirondelle* is there,
And also the laboratory, the strange heart of the ship
Uprooted, leaving red holes
In the deck that vanished in smoke.

Here are the trophies:
A walking stick made from the backbone of a shark;
Tortoiseshell combs, and fans of mother-of-pearl;
Corals that faded,
Losing the changing hues of sea and sky;
Sea shells under glass
That are as dull as buttons
Sewn on garments by girls who have faded.

The Philippine Islands are a box
And the smile of a lady in a mantilla.

A walrus stuffed with straw
Faces the diving helmet.
They remember Verdun and Passchendaele,
The mud-clouded wars of the ocean floor.

So all that oceanography, after all,
Was only a pawnshop.
For they brought home the tooth of the whale
And said, "Look!
It is only a doorstop, after all."

For Leviathan does not exist,
And the sea is no mystery.
For a shark is a walking stick.

And this we call the life of reason.

4

Idiots!
We too are all for reducing
The universe to human dimensions.
As if we could know what is human!

Just a few dippers of sea water
And a fair wind home . . .
Then surely we won't be destroyed.

A strange idea, if you consider
The dust of those settlements—
The parlors where no one lives;
The splinter that wounds the foot sole
On its way to the double bed;
And Leviathan over all,
The cloud shaped like a weasel or a whale,
Leviathan rising above the roof tops.

5

When men wanted the golden fleece
It was not wool they wanted.
They were the trophies that they sailed toward.

They were the sea and the wind
That hurled them over
Into the sea. They were the fishes
That stripped their thin bones. And they rose
In the night in new constellations.

They left no wreckage.
Nothing is floating on the surface.
For they yielded themselves
To the currents that moved from within.

They are mightily changed
In the corollas, the branched sea-heaven.

And you, my country,
These days your walls are moving,
These nights we are branching among the stars.

I say, but my mind is doubtful.
Are there any at sea?
If so, they have not whispered lately.

Frogs

The storm broke, and it rained,
And water rose in the pool,
And frogs hopped into the gutter,

With their skins of yellow and green,
And just their eyes shining above the surface
Of the warm solution of slime.

At night, when fireflies trace
Light-lines between the trees and flowers
Exhaling perfume,

The frogs speak to each other
In rhythm. The sound is monstrous,
But their voices are filled with satisfaction.

In the city I pine for the country;
In the country I long for conversation—
Our happy croaking.

My Father in the Night Commanding No

My father in the night commanding No
Has work to do. Smoke issues from his lips;
    He reads in silence.
The frogs are croaking and the streetlamps glow.

And then my mother winds the gramophone;
The Bride of Lammermoor begins to shriek—
    Or reads a story
About a prince, a castle, and a dragon.

The moon is glittering above the hill.
I stand before the gateposts of the King—
    So runs the story—
Of Thule, at midnight when the mice are still.

And I have been in Thule! It has come true—
The journey and the danger of the world,
    All that there is
To bear and to enjoy, endure and do.

Landscapes, seascapes . . . where have I been led?
The names of cities—Paris, Venice, Rome—
    Held out their arms.
A feathered god, seductive, went ahead.

Here is my house. Under a red rose tree
A child is swinging; another gravely plays.
    They are not surprised
That I am here; they were expecting me.

And yet my father sits and reads in silence,
My mother sheds a tear, the moon is still,
    And the dark wind
Is murmuring that nothing ever happens.

Beyond his jurisdiction as I move
Do I not prove him wrong? And yet, it's true
　　They will not change
There, on the stage of terror and of love.

The actors in that playhouse always sit
In fixed positions—father, mother, child
　　With painted eyes.
How sad it is to be a little puppet!

Their heads are wooden. And you once pretended
To understand them! Shake them as you will,
　　They cannot speak.
Do what you will, the comedy is ended.

Father, why did you work? Why did you weep,
Mother? Was the story so important?
　　"Listen!" the wind
Said to the children, and they fell asleep.

American Poetry

Whatever it is, it must have
A stomach that can digest
Rubber, coal, uranium, moons, poems.

Like the shark, it contains a shoe.
It must swim for miles through the desert
Uttering cries that are almost human.

The Inner Part

When they had won the war
And for the first time in history
Americans were the most important people—

When the leading citizens no longer lived in their shirt sleeves,
And their wives did not scratch in public;
Just when they'd stopped saying "Gosh!"—

When their daughters seemed as sensitive
As the tip of a fly rod,
And their sons were as smooth as a V-8 engine—

Priests, examining the entrails of birds,
Found the heart misplaced, and seeds
As black as death, emitting a strange odor.

Night Flowers

Leaves, what are you?

                  Flowers feed on me.

On a hill in Rome
There's my "Magnificent" with the red
Petals and white spike. In Tuscany
My "Passion." And in Paris
The orchid, blue, called by the inhabitants
"The Gendarme." I recall
The night I watered it with tears
In a room that smelled like humus.

And the cactus flowers of Monaco
On the violet-colored hill are unfolding
Near three nuns in their enormous hats
Poised on a rock like gulls or ships that sail
To Africa.

On the Lawn at the Villa

On the lawn at the villa—
That's the way to start, eh, reader?
We know where we stand—somewhere expensive—
You and I *imperturbes,* as Walt would say,
Before the diversions of wealth, you and I *engagés.*

On the lawn at the villa
Sat a manufacturer of explosives,
His wife from Paris,
And a young man named Bruno,

And myself, being American,
Willing to talk to these malefactors,
The manufacturer of explosives, and so on,
But somehow superior. By that I mean democratic.
It's complicated, being an American,
Having the money and the bad conscience, both at the same time.
Perhaps, after all, this is not the right subject for a poem.

We were all sitting there paralyzed
In the hot Tuscan afternoon,
And the bodies of the machine-gun crew were draped over the
    balcony.
So we sat there all afternoon.

The Riders Held Back

One morning, as we travelled in the fields
    Of air and dew
With trumpets, and above the painted shields
    The banners flew,

We came upon three ladies, wreathed in roses,
    Where, hand in hand,
They danced—three slender, gentle, naked ladies,
    All in a woodland.

They'd been to the best schools in Italy;
    Their legs were Greek,
Their collarbones, as fine as jewelry,
    Their eyes, antique.

"Why do lambs skip and shepherds shout 'Ut hoy!'?
    Why do you dance?"
Said one "It is an intellectual joy,
    The Renaissance.

"As do the stars in heaven, ruled by Three,
    We twine and move.
It is the music of Astronomy,
    Not men, we love.

"And as we dance, the beasts and flowers do;
    The fields of wheat
Sway like our arms; the curving hills continue
    The curves of our feet.

"Here Raphael comes to paint; the thrushes flute
    To Petrarch's pen.
But Michael is not here, who carved the brute
    Unfinished men."

They danced again, and on the mountain heights
    There seemed to rise
Towers and ramparts glittering with lights,
    Like Paradise.

How the bright morning passed, I cannot say.
    We woke and found
The dancers gone; and heard, far, far away
    The trumpet sound.

We galloped to it. In the forest then
    Banners and shields
Were strewn like leaves; and there were many slain
    In the dark fields.

Love, My Machine

Love, my machine,
We rise by this escape,
We travel on the shocks we make.

For every man and woman
Is an immortal spirit
Trapped and dazed on a star shoot.

Tokyo, come in!
Yuzuru Karagiri, do you read me?
San Francisco, darkest of cities, do you read me?

Here is eternal space,
Here is eternal solitude.
Is it any different with you on earth?

There are so many here!
Here's Gandhi, here's Jesus,
Moses, and all the other practical people.

By the light of the stars
This night is serious.
I am going into the night to find a world of my own.

Wind, Clouds, and the Delicate Curve of the World

Wind, clouds, and the delicate curve of the world
Stretching so far away . . .
On a cloud in the clear sight of heaven
Sit Kali and Jesus, disputing.
Tree shadows, cloud shadows
Falling across the body of the world
That sleeps with one arm thrown across her eyes . . .
A wind stirs in the daisies
And trees are sighing,
"These houses and these gardens are illusions."
Leaf shadows, cloud shadows,
And the wind moving as far as the eye can reach . . .

Walt Whitman at Bear Mountain

"... life which does not give the preference to any other life, of any
previous period, which therefore prefers its own existence . . ."

—ORTEGA Y GASSET

Neither on horseback nor seated,
But like himself, squarely on two feet,
The poet of death and lilacs
Loafs by the footpath. Even the bronze looks alive
Where it is folded like cloth. And he seems friendly.

"Where is the Mississippi panorama
And the girl who played the piano?
Where are you, Walt?
The Open Road goes to the used-car lot.

"Where is the nation you promised?
These houses built of wood sustain
Colossal snows,
And the light above the street is sick to death.

"As for the people—see how they neglect you!
Only a poet pauses to read the inscription."

"I am here," he answered.
"It seems you have found me out.
Yet, did I not warn you that it was Myself
I advertised? Were my words not sufficiently plain?

"I gave no prescriptions,
And those who have taken my moods for prophecies
Mistake the matter."
Then, vastly amused—"Why do you reproach me?
I freely confess I am wholly disreputable.
Yet I am happy, because you have found me out."

A crocodile in wrinkled metal loafing . . .

Then all the realtors,
Pickpockets, salesmen, and the actors performing
Official scenarios,
Turned a deaf ear, for they had contracted
American dreams.

But the man who keeps a store on a lonely road,
And the housewife who knows she's dumb,
And the earth, are relieved.

All that grave weight of America
Cancelled! Like Greece and Rome.
The future in ruins!
The castles, the prisons, the cathedrals
Unbuilding, and roses
Blossoming from the stones that are not there . . .

The clouds are lifting from the high Sierras,
The Bay mists clearing.
And the angel in the gate, the flowering plum,
Dances like Italy, imagining red.

Pacific Ideas—A Letter to Walt Whitman

When the schooners were drifting
Over the hills—schooners like white skulls—
The sun was the clock in that parlor
And the piano was played by the wind.

But a man must sit down,
And things, after all, are necessary.
Those "immensely overpaid accounts,"
Walt, it seems that we must pay them again.

It's hard to civilize, to change
The usual order;
And the young, who are always the same, endlessly
Rehearse the fate of Achilles.

Everyone wants to live at the center,
"The world of the upper floors."
And the sad professors of English
Are wishing that they were dead, as usual.

But here is the sea and the mist,
Gray Lethe of forgetfulness,
And the moon, gliding from the mist,
Love, with her garland of dreams.

And I have quarrelled with my books
For the moon is not in their fable,
And say to darkness, Let your dragon come,
O anything, to hold her in my arms!

Lines Written Near San Francisco

I wake and feel the city trembling.
Yes, there is something unsettled in the air
And the earth is uncertain.

And so it was for the tenor Caruso.
He couldn't sleep—you know how the ovation
Rings in your ears, and you re-sing your part.

And then the ceiling trembled
And the floor moved. He ran into the street.
Never had Naples given him such a reception!

The air was darker than Vesuvius.
"O mamma mia,"
He cried, "I've lost my voice!"

At that moment the hideous voice of Culture,
Hysterical woman, thrashing her arms and legs,
Shrieked from the ruins.

At that moment everyone became a performer.
Otello and Don Giovanni
And Figaro strode on the midmost stage.

In the high window of a burning castle
Lucia raved. Black horses
Plunged through fire, dragging the wild bells.

The curtains were wrapped in smoke. Tin swords
Were melting; masks and ruffs
Burned—and the costumes of the peasants' chorus.

Night fell. The white moon rose
And sank in the Pacific. The tremors
Passed under the waves. And Death rested.

Now, as we stand idle,
Watching the silent, bowler-hatted man,
The engineer, who writes in the smoking field;

Now as he hands the paper to a boy,
Who takes it and runs to a group of waiting men,
And they disperse and move toward their wagons,

Mules bray and the wagons move—
Wait! Before you start
(Already the wheels are rattling on the stones)

Say, did your fathers cross the dry Sierras
To build another London?
Do Americans always have to be second-rate?

Wait! For there are spirits
In the earth itself, or the air, or sea.
Where are the aboriginal American devils?

Cloud shadows, pine shadows
Falling across the bright Pacific bay . . .
(Already they have nailed rough boards together)

Wait only for the wind
That rustles in the eucalyptus tree.
Wait only for the light

That trembles on the petals of a rose.
(The mortar sets—banks are the first to stand)
Wait for a rose, and you may wait forever.

The silent man mops his head and drinks
Cold lemonade. "San Francisco
Is a city second only to Paris."

3

Every night, at the end of America
We taste our wine, looking at the Pacific.
How sad it is, the end of America!

While we were waiting for the land
They'd finished it—with gas drums
On the hilltops, cheap housing in the valleys

Where lives are mean and wretched.
But the banks thrive and the realtors
Rejoice—they have their America.

Still, there is something unsettled in the air.
Out there on the Pacific
There's no America but the Marines.

Whitman was wrong about the People,
But right about himself. The land is within.
At the end of the open road we come to ourselves.

Though mad Columbus follows the sun
Into the sea, we cannot follow.
We must remain, to serve the returning sun,

And to set tables for death.
For we are the colonists of Death—
Not, as some think, of the English.

And we are preparing thrones for him to sit,
Poems to read, and beds
In which it may please him to rest.

This is the land
The pioneers looked for, shading their eyes
Against the sun—a murmur of serious life.

NEW POEMS

The Union Barge on Staten Island

The crazy pier, a roof of splinters
Stretched over the sea,
Was a cattle barge. It sailed in the Civil War,
In the time of the Wilderness battles.
The beams are charred, the deck worn soft between the
    knotholes.

When the barge sank offshore
They drove the cattle on land and slaughtered them here.
What tasty titbits that day
For the great squawking seagulls and pipers!
A hooded shuffling over the dark sand . . .

Under your feet, the wood seems deeply alive.
It's the running sea you feel.
Those animals felt the same currents,
And the drifting clouds
Are drifting over the Wilderness, over the still farms.

Black Kettle Raises the Stars and Stripes

"Nits make lice," said Chivington.
"Kill the nits and you'll get no lice."

The white men burst in at sunrise, shooting and stabbing.
And there was old Black Kettle
Tying the Stars and Stripes to his tent pole,
And the squaws running in every direction

Around Sand Creek,
A swept corner of the American consciousness.

And it's no use playing the tuba to a dead Indian.

Columbus

To find the Western path,
Right thro' the Gates of Wrath . . .
—BLAKE

As I walked with my friend,
My singular Columbus,
Where the land comes to an end
And the path is perilous,
Where the wheel and tattered shoe
And bottle have been thrown,
And the sky is shining blue,
And the heart sinks like a stone,

I plucked his sleeve and said,
"I have come far to find
The springs of a broken bed,
The ocean, and the wind.
I'd rather live in Greece,
Castile, or an English town
Than wander here like this
Where the dunes come tumbling down."

He answered me, "Perhaps.
But Europe never guessed
America, their maps
Could not describe the West.
And though in Plato's glass
The stars were still and clear,
Yet nothing came to pass
And men died of despair."

He said, "If there is not
A way to China, one
City surpassing thought,
My ghost will still go on.
I'll spread the airy sail,"

He said, "and point the sprit
To a country that cannot fail,
For there's no finding it."

Straightway we separated—
He, in his fading coat,
To the water's edge, where waited
An admiral's longboat.
A crew of able seamen
Sprang up at his command—
An angel or a demon—
And they rowed him from the land.

The Laurel Tree

In the clear light that confuses everything
Only you, dark laurel,
Shadow my house,

Lifting your arms in the anguish
Of nature at the stake.
And at night, quivering with tears,

You are like the tree called Tasso's.
Crippled, and hooped with iron,
It stands on Peter's hill.

When the lovers prop their bicycles
And sit on the high benches
That look across to eternity,

That tree makes their own torsion
Seem natural. And so, they're comforted.

2

One of the local philosophers . . .
He says, "In California
We have the old anarchist tradition."

What can he mean? Is there an anarchist tradition?
And why would an anarchist want one?
O California,

Is there a tree without opinions?
Come, let me clasp you!
Let me feel the idea breathing.

I too cry O for a life of sensations
Rather than thoughts—
"The sayling Pine, the Cedar proud and tall."

Like the girls in our neighborhood,
They're beautiful and silent.

3

As I was digging in the back yard
I thought of a man in China.
A lifetime, it seemed, we gazed at each other.

I could see and hear his heart-beats
Like a spade hurling clods.
He pointed behind him, and I saw

That the hills were covered with armed men,
And they were all on the other side
Of the life that I held dear.

He said, "We are as various
As the twigs of a tree,
But now the tree moves as one man.

It walks. And the earth trembles
When a race of slaves is leaving."

4

I said, "Yet, all these people
Will fall down as one man
When the entrails of a bomb are breathing.

When we came down from Chosin
Carrying the guns in dainty snow-wear
And all the dead we had to,

It was a time of forgetfulness,
Like a plucked string.
It was a river of darkness.

Was it not so on your side, when you came
To the sea that was covered with ships?
Let us speak to each other,

Let the word rise, making dark strokes in the air.
That bird flies over the heads of the armed men."

5

One part of the tree grows outward.
The other I saw when, with a light,
I explored the cellar—shattering roots.

They had broken through the wall,
As though there were something in my rubbish
That life would have at last.

I must be patient with shapes
Of automobile fenders and ketchup bottles.
These things are the beginning

Of things not visible to the naked eye.
It was so in the time of Tobit—
The dish glowed when the angel held it.

It is so that spiritual messengers
Deliver their meaning.

Things

A man stood in the laurel tree
Adjusting his hands and feet to the boughs.
He said, "Today I was breaking stones
On a mountain road in Asia,

When suddenly I had a vision
Of mankind, like grass and flowers,
The same over all the earth.
We forgave each other; we gave ourselves
Wholly over to words.
And straightway I was released
And sprang through an open gate."

I said, "Into a meadow?"

He said, "I am impervious to irony.
I thank you for the word. . . .
I am standing in a sunlit meadow.
Know that everything your senses reject
Springs up in the spiritual world."

I said, "Our scientists have another opinion.
They say, you are merely phenomena."

He said, "Over here they will be angels
Singing, Holy holy be His Name!
And also, it works in reverse.
Things which to us in the pure state are mysterious,
Are your simplest articles of household use—
A chair, a dish, and meaner even than these,
The very latest inventions.
Machines are the animals of the Americans—
Tell me about machines."

I said, "I have suspected
The Mixmaster knows more than I do,
The air conditioner is the better poet.
My right front tire is as bald as Odysseus—
How much it must have suffered!

Then, as things have a third substance
Which is obscure to both our senses,
Let there be a perpetual coming and going
Between your house and mine."

Outward

The staff slips from the hand
Hissing and swims on the polished floor.
It glides away to the desert.

It floats like a bird or lily
On the waves, to the ones who are arriving.
And if no god arrives,

Then everything yearns outward.
The honeycomb cell brims over
And the atom is broken in light.

Machines have made their god. They walk or fly.
The towers bend like Magi, mountains weep,
Needles go mad, and metal sheds a tear.

*

The astronaut is lifted
Away from the world, and drifts.
How easy it is to be there!

How easy to be anyone, anything but oneself!
The metal of the plane is breathing;
Sinuously it swims through the stars.

Tonight the Famous Psychiatrist

Tonight the famous psychiatrist
Is giving a party.
There are figures from the sporting world
And flesh-colored girls
Arriving straight from the theater.

And many other celebrities . . .
The Jew looks serious,
Questioning, always questioning, his liberal error;
The Negro laughs
Three times, like a trumpet.

The wife of the host enters slowly.
Poor woman!
She thinks she is still in Hungary,
And clings to her knitting needles.
For her the time passes slowly.

Stumpfoot on 42nd Street

A Negro sprouts from the pavement like an asparagus.
One hand beats a drum and cymbal;
He plays a trumpet with the other.

He flies the American flag;
When he goes walking, from stump to stump,
It twitches, and swoops, and flaps.

Also, he has a tin cup which he rattles;
He shoves it right in your face.
These freaks are alive in earnest.

He is not embarrassed.
It is for you to feel embarrassed,
Or God, or the way things are.

Therefore he plays the trumpet
And therefore he beats the drum.

2

I can see myself in Venezuela,
With flowers, and clouds in the distance.
The mind tends to drift.

But Stumpfoot stands near a window
Advertising cameras, trusses, household utensils.
The billboards twinkle. The time
Is 12:26.

O why don't angels speak in the infinite
To each other? Why this confusion,
These particular bodies—
Eros with clenched fists, sobbing and cursing?

The time is 12:26.
The streets lead on in burning lines
And giants tremble in electric chains.

3

I can see myself in the middle of Venezuela
Stepping in a nest of ants.
I can see myself being eaten by ants.

My ribs are caught in a thorn bush
And thought has no reality.
But he has furnished his room

With a chair and table.
A chair is like a dog, it waits for man.
He unstraps his apparatus,

And now he is taking off his boots.
He is easing his stumps,
And now he is lighting a cigar.

It seems that a man exists
Only to say, Here I am in person.

The Tailor's Wedding

The room was divided by a curtain.
There was a space on the other side
Where the tailor lived and you waited.

There was a bed, a table, a basin.
The wall was covered with pictures of women—
Blondes, brunettes—a tailor's dreams—

And privation is shameless.
He had cut them out of the magazines
Carefully with a scissors.

At last the suit was altered.
When I counted out the *lire*
He was as silent as death.

The work was perfect—and cheap, considering
That the man's life came with it.

2

The interior of the room was as clear
As a glimpse of brain surgery.
I walked out, stunned, in the Italian sunlight.

And when I look back, the hero
Who lifts Medusa's head
Must yield to the tailor's scissors.

For he reminds me of days
When I was a student, and life
Out there—the light that hurt the eyes.

All day it was cutting and stitching
Ideas by a dim light—
Handwork, in an age of machinery;

While the streets belonged to the rich—
The people with strong teeth.

3

And women went with the rich—
With the smell of new car upholstery,
A wind, white tablecloths.

For the poor there are moving pictures,
From which the young man emerges
Drugged, to the harsh light.

The wires and boards of the electric signs
Are like the pallid structure
Of his own mind laid bare.

Yet, over the roofs of the city
The moon hangs, faithful to the last,
Revealing her amorous craters.

Muse of the city, hope of the insane,
What would he do without you?

4

Yet once, perhaps, in his wandering
He rooms with a poor family,
And there's a girl, the household drudge

With mop and bucket, always in a clatter.
She's always entering with "Please
Excuse me." It is she who penetrates

His disguise—he's not a student, but a hero!
On a cold night she brings him
A bowl of soup.

Her body is rancid and thin.
When he leaves for another town, she stands
At the door, convulsed in a handkerchief.

Dear heart, I have bestowed
Your hand on a skillful tailor.

5

Lightly I've gone through life, accepting
Their services—a soup bowl
And a suit of clothes.

In the door a handkerchief waves,
And the tailor turns away
Thinking—the thoughts that tailors have.

And so my real life, my feelings
Are left on the cutting-room floor
And swept away with a broom.

And I've come to the end of a street
That is full of strangers.
And still, a spot is gleaming—

Something like a handkerchief
Or a pair of scissors.

After Midnight

The dark streets are deserted,
With only a drugstore glowing
Softly, like a sleeping body;

With one white, naked bulb
In the back, that shines
On suicides and abortions.

Who lives in these dark houses?
I am suddenly aware
I might live here myself.

The garage man returns
And puts the change in my hand,
Counting the singles carefully.

Luminous Night

I love the dark race of poets,
And yet there is also happiness.
Happiness . . .

If I can stand it, I can stand anything.
Luminous night, let fall your pearls!
Wind, toss the sodden boughs!

Then let the birch trees shine
Like crystal. Light the boughs!
We can live here, Cristina,

We can live here,
In this house, among these trees,
This world so many have left.

In the Time of Villa

It was in the time of Villa
When they put me on trial—
"Tell us, what is it you do exactly
To justify your existence?"

They were shouting "To the wall!"
And I found myself standing against the wall.
Later I woke, when the stars
Were shining above the Plaza de Toros.

A column of ants passed by.
They stopped, surprised by a particle
Coming the opposite way . . .
Then turned around, in the new direction.

I heard some Indians talking . . .
Long ago, and yet it seems
Like yesterday.
And that is why, and why

I live by begging.
And it's not just for myself,
But the head and ears of the burro
Nodding against the stars.